STRIKETHRU

MY HISTORY OF FAILED RELATIONSHIPS

J.A. JERNAY

ISBN (electronic): 978-1-960936-62-2

ISBN (print): 978-1-960936-63-9

CONTENTS

EMOTIONAL BAGGAGE CHECK

Let me start by explaining what this book is not.

This isn't a collection of anecdotes about terrible first dates, though there are a few of those.

This isn't one of those trauma dumps either, where the author lays out all the people who ever wronged him and slays those dragons, one by one. I'm past most of that. It's true that some of the people in this book did me dirty, but mostly I try to explain why everything happened the way it did.

This also isn't a redemption story. If you want that, watch a rock-star biopic, or read the memoir of a high-profile drug addict.

But this is a story that I'm betting a lot of readers will see their own lives reflected in.

Strikethru is the story of my history of failed relationships—both friendships and romantic partners.

Some people shrug off failed relationships, give them no consideration. Out of sight, out of mind. They shouldn't. Nearly every happiness study ever conducted has found that the quality of a person's relationships determines his or her happiness, especially later in life.

This memoir is also part of an emotional journey that I've been on for the past decade. If you're like me, sometimes memories of people from your past will flicker around inside your head. I find myself analyzing how and why those relationships went wrong. Overall, it's created a bit of a conundrum. See, once you've committed to the path of emotional self-awareness, you start to see other people in high-definition resolution. It's like developing a sixth sense.

As a result, I often sense people's anxiety even when they're silent. I detect hyperindividuality in a person's choice of language and I have a pretty good idea what that says about that person's childhood. I know that procrastination goes hand in hand with perfectionism, and that perfectionism often means you had to earn a parent's love. I can even sometimes pick out people with borderline personality disorder in a crowd—they often have a distinctly vibrant and photogenic look.

All this kind of stuff also causes you to see loved ones in a new light. Sometimes this forces you to decide whether to help them or not. If so, that can cause new conflicts, because a lot of older people don't want to excavate issues from the past. They like to keep their past nasties locked in a box.

I used to be too open to others, but because of the experiences in this book, I've learned to close myself a bit more. It's as though I was handed a box of chalk, halfway through life, and told to start drawing protective circles around myself on the sidewalk.

This was a good thing. *Love like you've never been hurt before* looks sweet and nice when printed on a mug, but it isn't always good advice. Life is more complicated than that.

RELATIONSHIPS MATTER

Like other herd animals, we humans are designed to live in groups. Those groups regulate our blood pressure, our sleep cycles, our mental health, our emotional states. They also contribute to our longevity. Without a group, many of us feel depressed, anxious, or flatout weird. I'm no different.

But modern American civilization thinks it knows better. Our advanced technology has sold us the illusion that we are atomized and self-reliant. Because of our prosperity, we've decided that other humans are disposable meat sacks that are unnecessary to our happiness. It's a view of people as masses of mitochondria, and nothing more.

Even worse, we've decided to reorganize life around a brand-new interface: the screen. It's a cliché, but necessary to point out that the phone-based childhood has taken away all those biochemical cues that teens get from the physical presence of others. So now the younger generation is less socialized. You can see it in the way that many don't respond to social interaction, the way they avoid eye contact, the way they rarely meet friends in person, the way they move like ghosts through their environment. They spend their lives encased in media bubbles that they falsely believe cannot be penetrated.

This has been a long time coming. It didn't start with Generation Z, though they serve as a convenient whipping boy. *Bowling Alone*, by Robert Putnam, has had a place on my bookshelf for the last twenty years. First published in 2000, this book was built on a simple observation: People used to participate in group bowling leagues, but now they bowl alone. He applied that idea across the board, to every part of life.

Since that publication date, this trend has grown worse.

Thus, I've come to the unhappy conclusion that our biggest problem is too much individualism. It was a fancy and even radical philosophy back when Ralph Waldo Emerson sang the praises of living for yourself, alone. He even imagined himself as a lonely eyeball stomping across the fields of the nation.

Not anymore. You can draw a direct line from that philosophy to the screwed-up people waving their long designer fingernails on daytime talk shows. *I don't gotta do what anybody tells me, y'all ain't shit.* And we're not coping particularly well with it either. Humans are one of the few species whose members take their own lives, and our growing suicide rates reflect it.

———

IN MY FORTIES, I've learned a lot about my own relationships.

I've discovered that my own tendency to overcommitment and loyalty caused problems in relationships, mostly because I didn't let people go. Think of me as Pepe le Pew, with the cat struggling to escape my skunky grasp. I've also expected that same level of loyalty from others, which is hopeless.

I've also found that I've dated a lot more than most other men, for better or for worse. While they haven't succeeded as much as I have, they also haven't failed as spectacularly as I have. This has given me a richer, broader set of experiential data to analyze—though not as much as the founder of the OkCupid dating sites revealed in his excellent short book, *Dataclysm*.

Let me make one thing clear: I'm not the villain in these relationships. In most of these failures, I hung on too long, tried too hard, or cared too much. The other person, in most instances, distanced herself or himself from me. If anything, I let too many terrible women into my life and hung onto them for too long. I stayed too open to danger, with too few defenses.

By age forty, I had the scars to prove it.

In the last few decades, I've lived in six different cities in the United States. I've unfortunately become somewhat expert in navigating through new social groups. Most adult men don't stick their necks out for new relationships nearly as much as I have; most of us try to stay with the same trusted social group we had in our early twenties. Thus, as people get married and start popping out babies, the men end up bowling alone.

This book is addressed to anybody who has found themselves in the same boat.

3

THE NOT-SO-GREAT AMERICAN ROAD TRIP

Three months, thirty-nine states, and fifteen thousand miles of asphalt.

It was the ultimate summer road trip across the United States. I had a few thousand dollars, a tent, a sleeping bag, a map, a few travel guides, and a will to drive.

I also had a girl. Her name was Lilith, a blonde who'd just finished her master's degree at Johns Hopkins and who wanted an adventure before she settled down to her new engineering job in California in the fall.

The only thing I didn't have was a sexy red convertible. Instead, I made do with a gray Oldsmobile sedan inherited from my grandfather. Let's say it was reliable, and leave it at that.

I too had decided to move to California later that year. I'd chosen to head to Los Angeles to pursue screenwriting opportunities. I knew that I would stay there for long time, so it was important that I get some miles under my feet and adventure out of my system before hunkering down. There was a lot of the United States that I'd never experienced, including nearly everything west of the Mississippi.

Lilith and I traveled cheaply. For months, we slept in campgrounds, cheap motels, and a lot of friends' couches. At university, Lilith had collected male admirers the way that other people collect stamps. She'd even made cute calendars of the sexy men of the engineering department.

So, in nearly every state we visited, there was a different young engineering nerd waiting for us in his home with an extra bedroom prepared. Each one looked crestfallen at seeing me walk through the door. I don't think she'd told any of them about her male accomplice on her travels.

There were a lot of highlights. In the desert of west Texas, at Big Bend, we swam across the Rio Grande to Mexico and walked up a donkey path to a small *pueblito* for a beer at a concrete block shack. In southern Utah, we went a week without showering while clambering among the red rocks and slot canyons. In Oregon, we partied with radical leftists at a funk club. In the fields of Iowa, we stayed with a family of stodgy conservative farmers and challenged their boys to corn-eating contests. And in Maine we spent a week in a large summer house with Lilith's extended family, right on the Atlantic coast, fifteen people I didn't know, all eating pots of clams for dinner and throwing bits of saltwater taffy into each other's mouths.

I also learned a bitter lesson: Vet your travel partners carefully.

———

See, I knew Lilith, but I didn't *know* her know her—if you get the distinction. And her behavior grew difficult as the weeks went on. I began to see emotional damage that she'd kept hidden since we'd met a couple years earlier.

The big problem was that Lilith had zero conflict-resolution skills. She started fights with no clear intention of ever concluding them. Add to that my natural stubbornness, and the disagreements dragged on for hours, or days.

The weird thing was that, after the fight ended, she would calmly state that we hadn't been having a fight.

"If that wasn't a fight," I would say, "then what was that?"

"It was a discussion," she would reply.

I remember feeling a weird chill go down my neck. A UN peacekeeper could've recognized that we'd been fighting. An earthworm could've spotted it. This redefinition was a supreme bit of gaslighting, on her part.

On one occasion, I grew supremely annoyed with her and dropped her off at a campground and drove away. I left her there for five hours, alone. I don't apologize for that; she was acting that terribly, and there was nothing that could've placated her demons. At other times, her emotional dysregulation grew so hideous that I threatened to quit the trip completely, put her on a plane, and send her back to New Hampshire.

I searched for a good way to end her arguments in a civilized manner. I did find the kill switch, but it wasn't pretty. I started talking to Lilith in a quiet voice about how her father had abandoned her as a child, how he'd done the very best he could, how everybody deserves a good childhood but not all of us get them. This would shut her up. She would stop fighting, start crying, and then fall asleep.

I don't apologize for doing this either. Manipulation was the only way to stop her madness.

Prior to the trip, two mutual friends had quietly warned me about her, but I'd brushed them off. This overconfidence hurt me. It wouldn't be the last time.

In retrospect, I'm also amazed at how little money we

spent. The whole trip cost me about $3000 total. That's a thousand dollars per month. I also was proud of the fact that I'd seized the moment. I thought I might never have this type of opportunity for extended travel again.

I was wrong about that—but I would wait nearly fifteen years to find out.

———

A MONTH after the journey ended, Lilith and I joined forces once again to share a moving van out to the West Coast. We argued most of the way, and after arriving in southern California, we immediately settled fifty miles apart and mostly tried to forget about one another. I went my way, and she went hers. We talked on the phone now and then.

The next year, I extended an olive branch and asked her if she wanted to come with me to a U2 concert at the Staples Center. It was the Elevation tour, and I knew she was a fan. She agreed, and the night went off smoothly. A few months later, I drove the fifty miles down to her house to pick up some photos that she'd taken on our road trip. We laid on our stomachs on her bed, looking at the stacks of her high-quality shots of the Utah landscape, roadside shacks in Mississippi, odd people in public areas. I've never been much for taking photos, or for posing in them, and I admire people who shoulder that responsibility.

In an unguarded moment, Lilith admitted that she'd been "crazy" the previous summer. She used that word exactly. I felt relieved to know that I hadn't been over-reacting.

In the next two years, we talked a couple more times on the phone. During our final conversation, she told me that she was moving to Philadelphia, back on the east coast, thousands of miles away. She told me she hated engineering and was going to take her visual art seriously. It wasn't surprised. I told her to keep in touch.

Then she completely disappeared from my life.

Since then, a Google search tells me that she's become a visual artist focused on interpreting her trauma through oil and watercolor canvases. According to her biography at an art gallery, she is "haunted by memories of repeated child-hood sexual assault" and "other abuse, too, by family and others".

If she's telling the truth—and I think she mostly is—Lilith never revealed any of that to me. Even if she had, I don't know what I could've done. At age twenty-four, I was unaware of just how many women are affected by sexual abuse, including my own family members. Today, I can recognize the signs. Today, I would've spotted that trauma in her right quick.

My three-month summer road trip was strong in ambi-tion and planning but flawed in its execution. I don't regret it, but looking back, I would've chosen a different travel partner. I suspect Lilith might say the same about me.

4

BRIAN IN MICHIGAN

If friendship is a flower, ours lived for seventeen years. It was planted and blossomed in the Midwest, before being transplanted to California. There it died, like so many people's dreams.

But this wasn't a dream. Brian was real, and he was my best friend for a long time.

We met in sixth grade when we briefly went to the same middle school. There were a lot of differences between us. I was Catholic, he was nonreligious Protestant of some kind. I was a soccer player; he wasn't athletic.

We came from different socioeconomic backgrounds. My family was upper-middle class—my dad was a criminal defense attorney, my mother a civil servant—while his family was working class. His dad labored second shift in a factory and literally carried an old-fashioned lunch pail. Brian's mom was a part-time vet tech with a big bouffant hairdo that never seemed out of place. My parents had four college degrees between them; his parents had none.

I enrolled in a private Jesuit high school with a reputation for academic rigor. It produced students who were a bit too clever for their own good. Brian, meanwhile, went to a local public school with an ordinary reputation. I loved my high school, but he seemed unmoved by his own.

My family home was a Tudor-style subdivision home built in the early 1980s. It had four bedrooms and three baths and two sliding glass doors that opened onto a large elevated wooden deck that overlooked a public golf course. Brian's family home, on the other hand, was a century-old two-story house that sat a few feet from the edge of a major road. Traffic constantly zoomed past his living room, and sitting there, you just learned to shut out the noise. The house only had one full bathroom, and it didn't even have a shower—the whole family shared a single claw-footed tub. He didn't have the opportunity to bathe too much and sometimes had body odor as a result. The house didn't have central heating either. They fed chopped timber into a vintage cast iron wood-burning stove in the back room. It smelled cozy but was unbelievably inefficient. I can still feel how freezing his second-floor bedroom was in the winter.

———

STILL, we did have a lot of things in common, and the overlapping middle of our Venn diagram was enough to bind us together for a long time.

What stood out, then and now, was Brian's intelligence. He was smarter than both his parents put together. Possessed by a highly analytical mind, Brian loved to talk about the interactions of humans with their technological environments, which rubbed off on me. He had a great sense of musical pitch and sang much better than I could.

He was friendly too—everybody always welcomed him socially, more than they did to me, if I'm being honest.

As we grew older, I noticed something else: Brian needed to do better than his parents. He never said it out loud, but I sensed it underneath all his actions. He did in fact become the first person in his family to earn a bachelor's degree, and then the first one to earn a master's degree, both in engineering. I was proud of him for that, but I don't think I ever told him so.

What we had in common was that our energies matched perfectly. We were opposites. I was the active one who cooked up the ideas, while laid-back Brian was game for almost anything I suggested. At my worst, I could be demanding and judgmental, like some of my family members. At his worst, Brian could be lazy and dissociated, like some of his family members.

But these qualities fit together well.

We were the same height, same build, same hairstyle. We lived very close—I could bike over to his house in three minutes. And after that one semester in sixth grade, we never went to the same school again. This ironically helped our friendship. I knew some of his school buddies, and he knew a few of mine, but overall we never had any interference from other people in our relationship.

Brian let me indulge in the impatient side of my personality. I tend to get bothered by a lot of dumb things, like late-afternoon sunlight in my eyes. Once I threw my badminton racket at him after he beat me in a tense match, which clearly pissed him off. I apologized a lot for that. Other than that, I honestly can't remember anything that ever bothered him.

I used to think of us as kinetic energy and potential

energy. He would act, but only when acted upon, often by me. Stimulus and response.

Our peculiar dynamic worked well for a long time.

———

THE YEAR 1991 was a watershed year for rock music. The list of classic rock albums that were released from January to December of that one year reads like a list of greatest hits of the genre. Here's a partial list:

- *Nevermind*, by Nirvana
- *Ten*, by Pearl Jam
- *The Black Album*, Metallica
- *Use Your Illusion I & II*, Guns 'n' Roses
- *BadMotorFinger*, Soundgarden
- *Blood Sugar Sex Magik*, Red Hot Chili Peppers
- *Achtung Baby*, U2
- *Gish*, Smashing Pumpkins
- *For Unlawful Carnal Knowledge,* Van Halen

There were other great releases that year too, by Dire Straits, Rush, The Pixies, Lenny Kravitz, Primus, Ozzy Osbourne, R.E.M., and more. For anybody who was a fan of rock at that time, you were living in a golden era without knowing it.

For me and Brian, it was our tenth and eleventh grade years.

Until then, I'd listened mostly to other types of music—pop, disco, funk, R&B. My first concert, age five, was Lou Rawls. Thanks to my older cousin, who was a professional pianist, I'd been absorbing Rachmaninoff's 2nd Piano Concerto. He'd also introduced me to jazz giants like Oscar

Peterson. I even had a weird interest in gospel music. On a family trip to the New Orleans Jazz Fest, I spent an entire afternoon in the black gospel tent, a twelve-year-old white kid, alone, totally entranced by the singing, the shuffling, the people clapping in the aisles. I loved the energy.

I *still* love a good gospel tent.

As a kid, I thought that eighties rock was kind of a joke. Poodle hair and power chords looked and sounded stupid to me. The only exception was Def Leppard. Brian and I built music producer ears together. I used to put *Hysteria* on my CD player and we'd try to count the number of guitars on each song, then compare that with the number of guitarists in the band, to see how many tracks they'd recorded. Years later, it was a small vindication to hear the brilliant guitarist John Mayer plant his flag on the same hill, calling Def Leppard the best of that genre.

Musically, Brian and I had a few small differences. He liked Motley Crüe more than I did. He cranked up the *Dr. Feelgood* CD on his sound system before his Christian conservative dad got home from the factory. On the other hand, I liked the mellower Don Henley and Bruce Hornsby, who he didn't care for.

Then came 1991. And with it came nineties rock.

Brian and I were floored by the first Pearl Jam album. *Ten* seemed raw and incredible to both of us, way better than Winger or Poison or whatever sappy rock ballads were polluting MTV before that. Though Metallica's early thrash stuff wasn't for me, their Black Album grabbed my ears and demanded listening. It was the first metal album that didn't give me a headache.

My overall favorite became U2. I'd discovered them at Brian's house a couple years earlier, when I saw his mom had left a cassette on the floor of their living room. It was black and white with a photo of four guys standing in a desert by a tree. I asked if I could borrow it. Soon I'd bought everything they'd ever recorded. Then, when *Achtung Baby* came out the same month I turned 16 years old, it stayed in my car's CD player for about half a year. I became obsessed with the band, their energy, their intelligence, their religious background. Their themes were my themes.

That same year, Brian and I started driving to rock shows in his red Firebird. We made sure to see all the big titans that were passing through the Detroit area—Dire Straits, Rush, others I've forgotten. Two years later, we even saw a reformed Pink Floyd, who played the entire *Dark Side of the Moon* album for the first time in two decades.

We caught the U2 Zoo TV tour the first time in the arena, and the second time in the stadium. I was blown away by their artistic statement. The Irish guys were doing full blown European performance art, and I was a thousand percent onboard. It's hard to believe that U2 is still going strong today, over thirty years later, still capturing songs now and then that sound inspired by a divine power. It's become fashionable to hate them, but that's natural for any artist who gets globally popular for too long.

Most memorably, we sneaked out to the famous Guns n' Roses-Metallica coheadlining tour. Knowing we'd be prohibited from going, we both told our parents that we were sleeping over at each other's house. Mine were the only ones that really mattered; Brian's parents were more *laissez-faire*.

So there we perched, in the upper deck of the Pontiac Silverdome, watching the fights and drugs and flesh and chaos in the audience on the floor. I loved Faith No More, who were the openers, and Metallica started their show with the late summer daylight still streaming into the stadium. Dressed in black, they chewed up the stage. Them boys were impressive then. After their set, during the long stage change, the stadium projected live footage of women in the audience flashing their boobs for the cameras. We were a pair of virgin teenage boys, so you can guess our reactions. It was a long celebration of tits. The parade of breasts went on for so long that even we started to get bored.

Guns n' Roses didn't even take the stage until midnight. A few minutes into the show, Axl Rose vomited during "You Could Be Mine", then threw the microphone about fifty feet in the air before stomping off stage. He didn't come back for twenty minutes. I thought he seemed mentally ill. We left before it was even over.

That tour grew worse. A week later in Montreal, Metallica's James Hetfield burned himself on pyrotechnics, cutting their set short. Then Axl pitched another hissy fit and cut the Guns n' Roses set short too. Over two thousand people rioted and caused a million dollars of damage to the venue.

———

ROCK CONCERTS WERE FUN, but summers up north were the best times Brian and I ever had.

Ernest Hemingway wrote about fishing and trapping in the woods of northern Michigan in his first short-story collection, *In Our Time*. Our experience wasn't quite the same, eighty years later, but it wasn't all that different either.

My family had a small cottage south of Alpena on the shores of Lake Huron. I'd been going up there since I was old enough to walk, and as a little kid I literally spent eight hours a day swimming and splashing and sailing in the open

water. My sister and I were permanently tanned and spent
so much time in the water that we never had to bathe or
shower. I built elaborate beach art sculptures out of drift-
wood. I sometimes found old waterlogged boards washed
up on the sand, remnants of the nearly one hundred ship-
wrecks located under the waters of Thunder Bay since the
nineteenth century. I peed almost wherever I wanted.

It was close to heaven.

Later, Brian's family bought a small trailer and plunked
it in the woods about an hour north of our place, in Presque
Isle. That area is even more beautiful.

By age thirteen, he and I had joined forces. Between the
two of us, we were always heading up to the beaches and
forests—at first with our families, later just the two of us in
his Firebird. We stayed in his family trailer, crashing on a
bunk if we were lucky, maybe a pullout futon, sometimes on
the floor or in a tent outside. We'd bring our mountain bikes
and strike out across Presque Isle, packing lunches and
finding singletrack and doubletrack paths to explore. We'd
strip down to our bathing suits, or even sometimes nothing
at all, and dip into Lake Huron wherever we wanted. We
swam in front of lighthouses, across harbors, in remote state
parks.

At night, we played cribbage or euchre in the trailer
with his mom, dad, brother, uncle, friends. Other nights, the
group of us went to have bonfires on the nearby rock
beaches. That's dark sky country—the stars there are some
of the clearest on earth. The intersection of earth, air, fire,
water feels primal. Once, we were treated to the green
fingers of the northern lights dancing overhead for nearly an
hour, which is uncommon at that latitude. It's the only time
I've ever seen them.

I remember riding through the forest at night, hanging

off the back bumper of his family's pickup truck by one foot and one hand, his younger brother at the wheel, age thirteen.

They were great times.

Now in my forties, I still call these places my summer favorites. But I don't go there with Brian anymore, because our friendship didn't last.

5

BRIAN IN COLLEGE

After high school, Brian and I barely saw each other for five years. He went to the University of Michigan, while I accepted a full scholarship to a university in Washington, D.C. There, I leapt on all sorts of big opportunities—study abroad at Oxford University, a master's degree concurrent with my bachelor's degree, and a couple of years working at *The Washington Post*.

It was a frantic period for me. You can read about these experiences in two of my other books: *The Oxford Diaries* and *Bold*, the companion title to this one.

At age twenty-two, I decided to ditch journalism and politics and begin to write books instead, which is all I really wanted to do. Meanwhile, Brian had a lease on a simple two-bedroom apartment on Huron Avenue in Ann Arbor. He needed a roommate while he finished the second year of his master's program in Industrial and Operations Engineering, a.k.a. "in and out easy" engineering. It focused mostly on ergonomics, the human side of technology.

Talking on the phone, Brian and I realized that I could return to Michigan and move in with him.

It was an easy decision. I needed a cheap place to live while I took a shot at becoming a novelist. He needed a roommate who he could trust and who wouldn't bother him. We both knew what we were getting with one another.

Mostly, we were right.

I quit my job at America's most famous political newspaper and returned to Michigan in June in a U-Haul. I moved my stuff into his apartment, and soon Brian and I had slipped back into some of our familiar competitive patterns. When we weren't working or studying or writing, we played a lot of table hockey at a local arcade. We went on long bike rides. We joined my sister and her friends at raves in abandoned factories in Detroit's abandoned industrial corridor. We helped clean out my miserable grandparents' house after my mother moved them to an assisted-living home.

But the most important addition to our life became Brian's new foosball table. It sat prominently in our living room. At five o'clock pm each day, he'd come home from classes or his job, and I'd stop writing. We'd strip down to our shorts, crank up electronic dance music, maybe the Crystal Method or Paul Oakenfold, and face each other across the green foosball table. Then we waged battle. They were the kind of testosterone-driven games you can only have in your early twenties.

Six months passed, and we both became ridiculously fast players. I found that barely controlled chaos worked better than precise strikes. Every game was a 51-49 split. Today, I still surprise people with my furious foosball game. They don't really expect it.

Our competitiveness even extended to eating. Brian and I had always enjoyed moments of competitive eating at buffets, but one week we decided to make a proper contest of it. I cooked mounds of spaghetti, and two friends came over with a food scale to measure the plates and serve as referees. We faced one another over our kitchen table. We both made it through three full plates, but the moment he took the first bite of the fourth one, I fell onto the floor and gave up.

————

But the first small cracks were forming between us.

We were twenty-three years old and had already embarked on different career paths. Me, I'd grown my hair out to shoulder length. It looked terrible, and only lasted a year, but I needed to let loose after a very intense five years earning two college degrees while working in the headquarters of national political journalism. I was pulling back from a life of striving for prestige. The hair represented a pivot to the personal, to the way of the solopreneur, of the freelancer, of the artist.

Meanwhile, Brian was going a different way. He was starting to lose his hair, which he always kept short, and he was mentally preparing to begin a strict corporate career in automotive engineering and design. When not in class, he was running tests on automobile dashboards and doors, analyzing how volunteer drivers interacted with them in prototypes.

We were becoming different. That was okay.

One of his friends, Jeff, didn't like me much, mostly because I was hooking up with Lilith, Jeff's ex-girlfriend, who was still hanging around that summer before she began her own master's degree at Johns Hopkins University. Jeff even falsely called me an alcoholic at one point, mostly out of jealousy. This situation made Brian uncomfortable too, because my success with women reminded him of his miserable luck in that department. I know that seeing this girl leap into my arms within a week of my arrival in his house made him feel bad about himself.

Truth be told, he'd been getting down on himself a lot anyways. This internal pressure came out in the form of anger, especially when he was drinking. To my surprise, my once-placid best friend would go around insulting people after two or three beers. "Fuck you, fuck you, fuck you," he said once at a party, jabbing fingers at guests. It wasn't for laughs, either.

Over time, this Jekyll and Hyde tendency grew stronger. I have many faults, but being a bad drunk is not one of them. Booze has always relaxed me, and at one time it even used to bring out my inner people-pleaser. So watching Brian become an angry beer lout was jarring. I'd thought we were on the same page.

"You should try to be nicer when you drink," I said to him once, watching him deep in his cups.

"I don't want to be nicer," he spat.

"But it's not attractive," I replied.

"It's really not," echoed Lilith, sitting nearby.

"I don't *care* if it's not attractive," he replied.

Fair. He knew his own mind. But I also knew the reason for his anger.

————

DURING OUR FIVE YEARS APART, Brian's parents had divorced. His unhappy mother had left his salt-of-the-earth factory-worker father for no reason other than boredom. My own mother had predicted the split. She'd noticed the way his mother primped herself while peeling out of her driveway in her sports car every morning.

I remember seeing the divorce papers on their kitchen table during a Christmas visit. With the ink barely dry on the documents, his mother had moved in with another man named Neil. This guy was—in Brian's words—an exact replica of his own father. I've never met Neil and cannot confirm, but it sounded like she'd traded in a Chrysler sedan for a Chrysler sedan. Same make, same model.

It made Brian furious. He identified strongly with his simple lunch-pail father. So he took the blow on the chin, just like his dad had. Call it a genetically inherited emotional glass jaw.

The whole thing made me sad. I'd always liked his dad, the way he moved and spoke deliberately, the way he did sit-ups during commercial breaks on television, the way he wore knee-high white socks to hide his varicose veins. He was slow but very sweet and trustworthy. Today, I know what he must've been feeling during the split.

But that's a story for an upcoming chapter.

6

BRIAN IN SOUTHERN CALIFORNIA

I couldn't find an agent for my first novel, mostly because it was awful. I left Brian's apartment a couple months before his graduation. We promised to stay in touch, and we did.

He relocated to Los Angeles that summer for his first professional job at a small human factors company in Torrance, California. He was hired to perform a variety of driving tests, especially on human interactions with automobile dashboards.

A year later, after a long detour in Florida, I arrived in Los Angeles to hack my way into the entertainment industry. I was one of the many hungry young lions prowling the plains of the Hollywood savannah.

Brian and his new roommate Daniel Frum, a coworker, saved my ass upon my arrival. Their stupendous gift was letting me sleep on their couch until I got my new life sorted. I told them I would be there two weeks, but it ended up being seven. Furthermore, through Daniel's friends, I found my first job in Hollywood as a professional script analyst, and I kept it for years.

I owe both of them for these kindnesses. Bigtime.

Once I found my own apartment, and my own work, I moved out. It was the week before my twenty-fifth birthday.

That's when our friendship entered its third and final phase.

————

I DIDN'T SEE it right away, but for the next four years Brian began an even steeper descent into a stew of bitterness, anger, and self-loathing.

Outwardly, he seemed happy, at least at the beginning. I lived next to Beverly Hills, in a neighborhood with the stupefyingly literal name of Beverly Hills Adjacent. Meanwhile, Brian lived in Palms, near Motor Avenue, about a mile from Venice Beach. If you know Los Angeles, you know that we were close to one another, and he was always game for meeting at bars, or hanging out at home, watching movies. We hit up concerts and went mountain biking, just like the old days, but this time the trails were in the millionaires' hills of Malibu. We even climbed Mt. Whitney together, the highest peak in the contiguous 48 states. (You can read about that in *Bold*, the companion memoir to this one.)

But underneath it all, Brian was beginning to hate himself.

It showed in his disregard for fashion. Outside of work, he regularly wore the same plebian workingman clothes that his uncle, a janitor in rural Michigan, might wear to a hunters' bar deep in the woods. Cheap washed denim jeans, off-brand running shoes, a themed t-shirt. I don't have a problem with those clothes, but you have to recognize when to wear them, and when not to.

Brian couldn't read the room.

For a young single guy going out in Los Angeles in the first decade of the new millennium, a typical outfit included shiny black shoes, slightly baggy dark jeans, a striped collar shirt, and frosted tips on your hair. I bought all the clothing but refused the peroxide. He, however, refused all of it. More than once, we were turned away from bars because of how he was dressed.

Once, he'd decided to head out for a night on the town wearing a pair of shorts. We were rejected everywhere we went.

I exploded at him. "You can't wear shorts when we go out to a nightclub in Los Angeles on a Saturday night!"

"Why not?" he said, wounded.

"You just can't! It's not how it's done in big cities! Look, I love up north rural Michigan too, but this isn't like that! You're with stylish people here! This is a sophisticated city!"

Unlike him, I'd already lived in the heart of a major metropolis, Washington, D.C. I'd worked at The Washington Post. I'd had experience with the ways of urban sophisticates as they virtue-signaled to one another. To Brian, a working-class Midwestern boy from simple people, this was all foreign territory.

"Why do people care how I'm dressed?" he said.

"Because first impressions are important," I said, forcing patience into my voice. "People judge you by your appearance. It isn't right, but it's the way it is. You have to put your best foot forward."

Brian looked glum. He'd been seeing a girl who'd just ghosted him that week.

"What's wrong?" I said.

"Why can't somebody just love me for who I am?" he said.

I didn't know how to respond at first.

"A woman *will* love you," I finally replied, "but to get to that point, you have to create attraction first. Clothing is a part of that."

Soon things grew worse. Brian started dating another girl, but he fell asleep on her sofa while waiting for her to get ready. She couldn't wake him up either, so she let him sleep. When he woke up hours later, they cancelled the date, and after that, she stopped returning his calls.

"You must've been tired," I said diplomatically.

"I don't know what happened," he confessed.

"Well, falling asleep on her couch doesn't give her the impression that you're ready to conquer the world."

"But I don't want to conquer the world!" he protested.

"That's fine," I replied, "but just don't let her know that, at least not right away."

On another occasion, he arrived home from work at six o'clock pm, parked his car in the garage, turned off the motor—and passed out asleep. Right there, in the driver's seat. He woke up nine hours later, at three o'clock in the morning, to the sound of his dog barking from his apartment above.

The problem is obvious in retrospect. Brian was suffering from depression. If I'd been more aware, I would've figured that out. But I didn't have that vocabulary back then. People in my extended family have experienced a lot of depression, and still do, but society didn't feel comfortable with that word until recently.

It's all different today. You can't throw a vitamin planner in the air without hitting someone on an SSRI. For better or worse, things have changed.

———

DURING THIS TIME PERIOD, one ray of sunshine entered Brian's life: his new roommate named Abby Lindquist.

A white girl from Minnesota, Abby was a dance instructor who taught in the LA public schools. She was our age, and she'd traveled through Africa for a year, learning different forms of dance, and sleeping with as many African guys as she could. I know that because she loved to tell me about her sexual adventures.

Sometimes Abby called me to go hiking together, when LA schools had a weekday off. She knew my schedule was flexible, so I'd pick her up and we'd go trekking on the mountain trails overlooking the Pacific. I diplomatically listened to her tell me about the various monster penises she'd enjoyed abroad. Abby was entertaining. I liked her as a sidekick, but romantically she was a no-go zone for about forty different reasons.

One of those reasons was her boyfriend, Dodzi. He was an immigrant from Ghana, working as a financial advisor downtown. Katy Perry wouldn't release "Hot N Cold" for a few years yet, but those two had that same drama—hot and cold, yes and no, in and out, up and down. I never knew their status, it changed so frequently. They'd argue, break up, get back together, have passionate makeup sex so loudly that Brian would call me to say that he couldn't sleep over the noise.

Still, Abby filled their apartment with life and love, plants and flowers. A woman's touch is a magical thing. They weren't dating, but she made Brian's home a better place than it had been with Daniel. Back then, I'd once found a bottle of 10W-30 motor oil stored in the kitchen cabinet next to their dinner plates.

Abby wore a constant smile on her face and a sparkle in her eye. She inspired Brian towards happiness.

Once, she invited me to go with her to a private performance of the Senegalese national dance troupe, which was
in Los Angeles while preparing for a big performance. They
were staying in somebody's house in Baldwin Hills, where
the African diaspora lives in Los Angeles. I'd already been
there for a cookout earlier, where I scorched the inside of
my mouth on some unnamed bright orange Ghanian hot
sauce that nobody wanted to touch, including the Africans.

Abby and I entered the living room and were greeted by
twenty African women and a few LA locals, all mingling.
There was only one other man in the room, a black American guy. Soon some Afropop music came on the speakers, a
chair was placed in the middle of the floor, and we sat in a
ring around it. Several Senegalese dancers took turns
working that chair like a part-time job. It wasn't twerking,
that doesn't do it justice—they were smashing it harder than
that. And their ass cheeks were as massive as their waists
were small.

Those are the kinds of places Abby liked to take me.

Brian, meanwhile, was slowly morphing into Eeyore.
His dancing grew so stiff and bad that I hesitated to ask him
to any more nightclubs. Another night, while out at a
Brazilian club in Palms with me and Abby and some others,
he put his head down on a table in a club and refused to
speak or move. On one occasion, I introduced him to a girl
I'd been dating, a singer and model, without realizing the
effect it would have on the way she perceived me. "Brian is
just sad," she messaged me later, before dumping me the
next week. She was haughty and self-absorbed, but in this
case, she was right. He was sad, in a few senses of the word,
and it made me look sad too.

In short, he'd started to become a liability. Even worse, I
was pulling the one-sided friendship along. I was calling

Brian twice a week or so, usually at home, sometimes at work. These were as much checkup calls as they were friendship calls. He seemed to welcome them, but I noticed that he never reciprocated.

———

THE DAY of the September 11 attacks provided another reveal.

My father woke me up with a phone call at about ten minutes before seven o'clock in the morning, telling me I had to turn on the television. I snapped on CNN to see the second tower falling into a pile of dust. Stunned, I sat on my sofa in my bathrobe, while my roommate Andy did the same. We couldn't move. Like everybody else, we were pinned to the screen.

Eventually, I opened the door to our apartment for anybody else in our courtyard apartment complex who wanted to stop by. One by one, our neighbors trickled in to chat and commiserate and watch the coverage. We became a small gathering of shock, sadness, and anger. It never occurred to me to go to work.

Around one o'clock that afternoon, I called Brian. He wasn't at home. So I called his work number. He picked up.

"Can you believe this?" I said.

"Believe what?"

"The terrorist attack in New York City," I said. "Hey, can I ask why you went to work?" In the entertainment industry, all the studios had shut down. In fact, most of the nation had shut down, out of shock and courtesy and security.

His voice grew tense. "It's just another day. Same as yesterday."

"No, it's not," I said. "This is different. This is like Pearl Harbor. This is a horrendous day in the history of our country. It's gonna change everything."

"Nope," he said. "It's just another workday."

"Fine," I said, "whatever."

I hung up.

I never thought Brian could be that insensitive, but this was proof that he was. I realize now that he'd built a mechanism to keep out any news that might challenge his shaky mental health. He was acting the way that a dry drunk does, strictly controlling his environment to keep himself from going off the rails.

———

LIFE CHANGED AGAIN when Abby announced that she was pregnant. Her boyfriend Dodzi was the father, and he was furious. I never found out exactly what transpired between them, but to nobody's surprise their storm and strife failed to magically resolve once she was with his child.

Abby's mother came and stayed in their apartment for a while during the pregnancy. I chatted with her, a middle-aged mother brimming with Minnesota nice. She told me that she was disappointed, that she couldn't believe her daughter had done something so impulsive as get knocked up by her on-again-off-again boyfriend.

I could believe it. Abby was one hundred percent female, in the anthropological sense. She operated according to the ancient dual mating strategy that some women have employed since the beginning of time—get pregnant with a perceived sexy man, then find a second man with more resources to raise the offspring.

Meanwhile, Brian was a bystander to the madness in his

own apartment. I wonder about his thoughts about his roommate expecting a baby. After all, he didn't need to live with her. He could've moved out, or he could've asked her to leave.

But he didn't.

————

ONE AFTERNOON, I was working at the desk in his bedroom while he was downstairs in the living room. I looked inside his papers and saw a handwritten essay in green ink on looseleaf. It was Brian's handwriting. I scanned the pages, quickly, in case he caught me snooping.

I realized that I'd stumbled onto his journal, and what he'd written was ugly. It was several pages of extreme self-hate, starting with blaming himself for his parents' divorce a decade earlier and proceeding to blame himself for going the last four years without having sex.

I read that last part twice, then a third time. Brian had never confided that in me. We'd talked about women a lot, but he'd kept the extent of his failure close to his chest.

Of all the women he'd tried to date, not one of them had decided he was worthy of sex? I can't imagine how badly that must've damaged a young man already struggling with cratering self-esteem.

Before that day, I'd thought Brian was a beta male. That term isn't meant to be critical or condescending. He was my best friend, a responsible wage-earner who made a better salary than I did. He helped people around him, to a fault. As the owner of a small truck, he'd assisted coworkers move apartments nearly every weekend, being too nice to ever tell anyone no.

There are millions of men like him everywhere. They

serve as the backbone of civilization. I salute all of them. Think how much better society would be if we produced more men like that.

But, on that day, I saw that was only half the story. I realized that he'd spiraled down, down, deep down into the grimy basement of anger and self-recrimination. He'd entered that bizarre subterranean place where men with emotional problems fold in upon themselves and become drawn towards cuckoldry, fetish, and kink. He hadn't written about those things in his short journal, not exactly, but I could read between the lines.

He had become what today we call an incel.

I couldn't help but think back to his parents. Brian's mother had been emotionally cold and distant to Brian. And that strange bouffant hairdo had never seemed to lose its shape. It wasn't until we were in our mid-twenties that Brian had off-handedly told me that his mother's hair was a wig. She'd lost all her hair as a teenager due to alopecia.

I'm not a therapist, so I'll let you draw your own conclusions about what kind of effect that could've had upon her ability to bond with her children. At the time, that was too big a question to consider, and I put it out of my mind.

———

I RESOLVED to help my best friend. I couldn't make him go to therapy, but I could help him in other ways.

My impatient mind kept circling back to his embarrassing clothing. While his work wardrobe was typical khakis and polos, the rest of his closet was growing worse. He'd begun wearing jean shorts with holes and rips and stains—and not in a fashionable way. I couldn't do much for his emotional state, I reasoned, but at least I could make him feel better about how he looked in the eyes of the world.

So I hatched a weird idea. I would perform a fashion intervention.

I called Abby and ran the idea past her. She agreed that it had to be done, though later Brian reported that she'd said the exact opposite to him. She liked to play both sides of the street. I also called Lilith and ran the idea past her as well. She enthusiastically agreed.

Maybe it was a good idea, maybe it wasn't. To this day, I'm not sure.

It proceeded exactly the way it sounds. With Abby's help greasing his psyche the night before, I went over to his apartment on a Saturday morning with three large cardboard boxes. I read a simple short statement to him that I'd written the night before. It was maybe four sentences. I don't recall what it said exactly, but it mimicked the language of addiction interventions: *your problem has negatively affected my life in the following ways, blah blah blah.*

He listened quietly. I could see he was holding back a lot.

"So what do you want to do?" he said.

"I want to ask your permission to go into your closet and remove the clothing that's causing a problem in your life."

He wasn't angry. It seemed like he'd halfway expected this. Soon he'd grudgingly agreed. I spent the next hour rifling through his clothes with him. I ended up removing most of his casual garments, leaving just his work clothes. He was upset but also oddly resigned to the process. I think he'd been waiting for someone to show some concern for him.

I told him I would keep the clothing at my house for a few days in case he changed his mind.

That night, he emailed me asking for a few pieces back. In the email, he added this:

One important note, you will never see me wearing any of the things you give back to me. You have made me irrevocably paranoid about anything I WEAR around you, and probably on a deeper level anything I DO around you.

That's what I was afraid of. Judge me if you want, but I crossed that line with full knowledge of the consequences. It was a necessary gamble; our relationship couldn't have continued the way it had been going. Socially, he'd become a heavy chain around my neck. Brian needed to become someone I could introduce to the people that I was meeting.

He'd guessed it too. Look at the next paragraph of his email:

"Why would he willing to do that?" I kept asking myself. The undeniable answer that I have arrived at is this: while you genuinely want to help me here, it is also as much about other people's perception of YOU when I'm around.

Brian was right. He was already at a social disadvantage in the fast Hollywood entertainment scene by being a white guy engineer from the Midwest. His clothing and demeanor weren't helping either. My loyalty had been stretched to its breaking point.

He ended the email positively: *I do fundamentally appreciate what you have done here; I just don't totally agree with the tactics or some of your responses.*

I suggested that we go shopping for new clothes together. To my surprise, he agreed, but only after the sting had worn off.

The next weekend, we met at the Beverly Center to select a mountain of new clothes. He was making at least sixty grand a year—a fortune back then—and with few bills to pay, he could afford a shopping spree. I helped him pick out new collar shirts, pants, shorts, and shoes. He dropped over a thousand dollars at Macy's in about two hours. And he seemed excited to do it.

Again, Brian contained a lot of potential energy. He just needed someone to prod him.

———

IN FOLLOWING MONTHS, he found a new girlfriend, and this one seemed to stick around for a while. However, Brian never let me meet her, which didn't surprise me. His communication began to taper off too. I guess that he was finally getting laid, courtesy of his new clothes. Or maybe something else had snapped.

It was hard to say, since he wasn't talking.

Months passed. I stopped calling and leaving messages, because he never replied. He did send an email every few weeks. Keep in mind that we only lived two miles apart, and we'd once been best friends.

He who cares the least controls the relationship, and Brian was in control.

I found out from mutual friends that he'd been cutting other people out of his life, left and right, including his former roommate and coworker Daniel Frum. That was a surprise. For the last four years, Brian had halfway worshiped Daniel, who was socially smooth and had a fiancée who everybody but me seemed to believe was a sterling example of perfect womanhood. I'd noticed that Brian even unconsciously imitated the way Daniel stood, spoke, and laughed.

I picked up the phone and called Lilith again, who knew a totally different set of Brian's friends than I did, people who lived down in Orange County. We began to compare notes. Lilith told me that Brian had been ruthlessly ending friendships with people in that group too. Then she told me that he'd coldly dumped that new girlfriend, the one I'd never met, devastating her so badly during the breakup that the girl had packed up her stuff, ended her lease, and moved out of Los Angeles. I counted four people I knew that he'd cut ties with; Lilith said she could count at least five more. Nine people total, and that wasn't including us. He'd mostly stopped communicating with her too.

I saw the writing on the wall. Brian was fighting an internal revolution, and he was leading all his friends to the guillotine, one by one.

The only reason he hadn't dumped me directly, I think, was the length of our relationship. At that point he was 29 years old, and I was 28. We'd known each other for 17 years, more than half our lives. For many years, we'd been best friends. We weren't anymore, and probably hadn't been for a while, in his mind.

I sighed, thanked her, and hung up. I knew what I had to do.

It was the first week of November, and my birthday was the following week. I'd wait to see if he'd acknowledge it, or message me, or do anything at all.

No word came until the night before my birthday, when he sent me an email, which I didn't see until the next day. It read—

SUBJECT: *I'm a douche*
   Yeah, I most certainly am a douchebag.
   I apologize for falling so far out of touch. I feel awkward now trying to meekly get back in touch. So awkward that I

didn't want to call you out of the blue, especially on your
bday.

So, happy bday! Not sure what you might be doing
tomorrow, but considering my ineptitude at friendship I
certainly understand if you don't want me around. Espe-
cially considering that we have not talked in a couple
months.

Sorry man.
-B

I NEEDED A REAL FRIEND, and this wasn't that. I honestly wasn't sure what this message even was. A miserable attempt at a half-assed relationship? It felt like an imposter had written it.

I knew what this meant, however. A couple days later, I replied with my own email. I told him that our friendship was over, but if that if he ever wanted to restart it, I'd love to talk.

I let him go. That was what Brian really wanted, deep down. He needed to be free of me—and of many other people too. He needed to reinvent himself. Depression pushes people to extremes.

He never replied to my email. As of this writing, that was twenty years ago.

———

I STAYED in touch with Abby for a while afterwards. She and Brian went their separate ways after her baby was born, but the following summer, I met Abby and her new infant at a world music festival in downtown LA.

I dandled the tiny girl on my lap while Abby caught me

up on my former friend. Brian had evidently suffered a near-total meltdown and quit his job. He switched to a different automotive company that required him to go out to a testing track in the desert, somewhere near Palmdale. He'd moved to a farflung apartment in Sylmar, in the north San Fernando Valley. There, according to Abby, he'd found a new girlfriend who now ran his life, which included dressing him in Seven jeans (the most fashionable brand then) and slick shoes.

"He looks so good now!" she said. "When I saw him, I was like wow!"

"I'm happy for him," I muttered.

Abby then mentioned that Brian had referred to me as "Mister Hollywood". That didn't make much sense. I worked *in* Hollywood, but I wasn't *of* Hollywood. Those weird people were dysregulated emotional wrecks, cluster-B time bombs. My own attachment style was as secure as it comes. In fact, I was growing annoyed with playing horseshit Hollywood games and was already sliding out the industry.

Couldn't Brian see that? I guess not. To him, I'd been consorting with the enemy—the shallow, exploitative snakes of Hollywood. To him, I'd obviously turned my back on everything I'd ever been.

That was wrong. But maybe he needed to turn me into a boogeyman.

I knew then that I'd made the right decision in ending the friendship. I mentioned to Abby that I was transitioning into educational work, hoping that word would get back to him, so he could stop falsely painting me in his mind as something I wasn't.

———

IF YOU'RE an astute observer of human nature, and if I've done my job with this part of this book, you've probably already guessed how this story ends.

A few months later, my phone rang. I saw it was Abby and picked up. She was calling to see how I was doing.

"I'm fine," I said.

"Are you still with that girl? What was her name?"

"Fang," I said. "She's great. How's Dodzi?"

"We broke up," she answered calmly. "I think he's going back to Africa or something. I don't know."

Nothing about their relationship surprised me. She'd probably give me a different answer tomorrow. "That's too bad," I said.

"It's okay," she replied. "Anyways, I'm seeing somebody else."

"Oh yeah? Who?" Abby was now a single mom on the prowl.

"Brian," she said.

I couldn't speak for a moment. "You and Brian are dating?"

"Yeah, of course! Why not?"

"Well, the timing is strange—"

She went on, justifying her decision to start a love affair with her former roommate and my former friend. It really wasn't needed. I wasn't judging. All I could think was that she was fulfilling the second half of the ancient dual-mating strategy. She'd found a reliable man with resources to raise the baby that she'd let the sexy man plant in her uterus.

We hung up, and I stared at the phone for a while, not knowing how to feel.

It was the last time I ever spoke to her.

———

SHE AND BRIAN moved in together, as lovers, shortly afterwards. And there my direct information stops, except for what I've gleaned from mutuals and online. Brian and Abby have been a couple for nearly twenty years now. He's taken Abby's daughter as his own. The baby that was conceived in his own apartment. He might've even listened to it happening, another man jamming his cock into his future wife's vagina.

I wouldn't have accepted those terms. But he did. Maybe it seemed like a good deal for a man with self-esteem so low that he was grateful for any scrap of acceptance that a woman tossed at him. From my current viewpoint, Abby looks a lot like a female who recognized that her roommate would make a terrific provider, and who slithered into his life when she needed his money most.

But if they're happy together, then who am I to judge?

She gave Brian his own child too, another girl. In his career, Brian has become a full-on company man, as predicted. He has spent the last seventeen years as a manager at a major Asian automobile manufacturer. He and Abby left Los Angeles behind and now live in Orange County.

After our breakup, Brian and I lived together in the same state for another decade. Yet we never spoke or saw one another again.

———

WOULD I have done anything differently to save our friendship?

Maybe I could've skipped the fashion intervention, but I don't think that would've made a difference in the outcome. Something had to end our relationship. We were two tectonic plates that fit together for a long time, but then we started to move past one another. The resulting earthquake was inevitable, one way or another.

Today, I imagine that we have little to nothing in common. I've changed a lot, especially after my divorce. I've become a world traveler who's lived abroad for years, who's fully fluent in Spanish, who's a twenty-year veteran of the freelance education game, who's written or contributed to nearly a hundred books.

He probably wouldn't know what to think of any of that. Brian's a nine-to-six company man with two kids and a commute.

The sad truth is that our Venn diagram no longer overlaps, not the way it used to. Brian is a convergent thinker who's apparently lived a conventional but rewarding life. I'm a divergent thinker who's danced along the edges of a life of risk. (See *Bold*, the companion memoir to this one.)

The truth is that I was a bit of a handful during that period in my life too. While I was aware of people's emotional states, I was also demanding, including of him. The years from ages 23 to 28 were the most difficult of my life, hands down, and Brian got the distinct pleasure of enjoying me during that period. If I were to change anything from that time, it would be to talk less and judge less, and to listen more and understand more.

It probably wouldn't have made a difference to the endgame, since so few friendships last a lifetime, but that's what I would've done.

7

DATING IN LOS ANGELES

If you ever met my parents, you might wonder where the hell I came from. I don't particularly resemble either one. This has been brought up many times, by many people, in many places.

My dad was born on the cusp of the Silent Generation, a fact that basically defines him. Khaki pants. Lands' End catalogs. He doesn't much care about emotions, or music, or travel. He's a terrible listener. The two things he really likes are NCAA basketball and Slavic history. He's an anchor of a man, solid, maybe too solid—there is nothing fluid about him. He'll never disappoint you, but he'll never try to impress you either. He sees no point in gift-giving. He prunes bushes with shears. These days, he doesn't say much anymore. I love him though.

As of this writing, he's been married to my mother for 55 years. She's more assertive, more risk-taking, and much more bull-headed. As a mental health responder for the American Red Cross, she was deployed to 17 different disaster zones. This was during her sixties. In the same period, she pulled herself out of a frozen lake after plunging through the ice trying to rescue a drowning dog. Her stories are wild and improvised and she can't always separate fact from fiction. I love her too.

My father and mother were married at ages 23 and 22, respectively. They've worked hard to build a life together, and like most people of that time, they had a strong tailwind their whole lives.

Armed with their example, I arrived in southern California, a lamb to the slaughter.

————

PICTURE IT: A young, tall, single guy in a metropolis filled with gorgeous women. Filled with optimistic energy, I was excited to see what type of fish I could haul into my boat.

Well, my first year in California was the longest dry spell of my entire life. I soon discovered that dating in LA is life on hard mode. Surrounded by thousands of beautiful but emotionally damaged people, all trying to get ahead in the entertainment industry, I went on a lot of dates with no success.

I once took a long drive to Redondo Beach to meet with a redhead who worked in an autism clinic; she stood me up. I met up with a schizophrenic girl on disability whose face was perpetually frozen in a flat affect. I did my best with the attractive waitress at an English pub in Santa Monica who was also a writer, like me, but she was so unhappy with her life that she rendered herself undateable.

In a city of twelve million people, you can go on dozens of terrible first dates. I did exactly that—over eighty of them in five years. It was like a sport.

There was a gorgeous British actress who'd had a role on *Seinfeld*. She was also a vegan, a yoga teacher, and an amateur numerologist. She told me that my birthdate made me a portal to another dimension. I asked for the check after twenty minutes, beauty be damned.

Or the Vietnamese girl who showed up for our date with a large wildcat on a leash. It was a half wild African cat, and she was breeding it for profit. "She thinks her name is *beautiful* because that's the only word people say to her," she remarked. After coffee, she suggested taking the animal for a walk. I took the leash and ended up pulling that wildcat down from trees, hauling it out of sewers, dragging it across lawns and driveways. Later I discovered the girl had a message on her answering machine saying, "Herpes is like a box of chocolates, you never know what you gonna get." Fortunately things hadn't progressed that far, and I saw myself to the exit.

Some were brushes with celebrity. I had a weird two-week flirtation with Leonard Cohen's daughter, who it turned out was totally mental and sabotaged the relationship. There was a pair of unsuccessful dates with a producer of the movie *Idiocracy*. Call me not sure, but I wanted to make doubly sure that we were wrong for one another.

Once, I was seated next to a beautiful buxom blonde on my flight from L.A. to Detroit. We hit it off, I snagged her number, and later asked her out. The date was a disaster. When I tried to kiss her, she swiveled her head so that all I got was a mouthful of hair. At the end, as I dropped her off in front of her apartment, she threw a condom at me before she exited my truck. "At least I gave you something," she spat.

That was all just in the first year. I was a nobody in his

mid-twenties, invisible to women. My position was low on the totem pole; as a script analyst, I was bottom of the Hollywood studio food chain. I'd had a lot of career success early on, so in retrospect it was good to be force-fed a heaping plate of humility.

While Brian had been pulling away from me, I'd been drawing closer to a new friend.

His name was Casey Carter, and he was my new roommate.

My previous roommate, Noah, had gone broke trying to commute between LA and Chicago to take care of his severely ill father. So he'd given up his half of our apartment and begun couch-surfing. I bade goodbye to him and found myself on the market for a new living partner.

Exactly two blocks away I found Casey, also looking for a new roommate. He already had a lease on a much nicer apartment than mine, with a big balcony and a wet bar. He was two years older than me, an inch taller at 6'3", and single. He was also a California native.

We shook hands and hit it off right away. He showed me his apartment, we chatted, and in less time than an episode of a sitcom we'd agreed to live together. It was a very male decision: a few words, implicit trust, and quick action. I loved that I could stay in the same neighborhood too. He lived only about three hundred meters away.

After a quick three-hour move the following weekend, my life continued as before.

———

CASEY BOASTED a big mop of black curls and a tall, lean frame. He was gentle and listened carefully to people. He never, ever raised his voice or interrupted anybody. Our energies matched well, as he found my semi-comedic musings about life funnier than they probably were. He also appreciated the fact that I handled my money well regarding rent and utilities and food. I sometimes cooked dinner for both of us, just to be welcoming.

But Casey wasn't your typical single guy in LA for one reason: He was a heterosexual man who worked in interior design. This is unusual. Most men in that field are LGBTQ. His boss, Jonathan, spent most of his time catering to wealthy entertainers, and he himself was gayer than a bouquet of lilies in April. Design people all over the west side of LA therefore assumed his handsome younger assistant was too.

But Casey was *very* hetero—and way more active than me in that department. Women found him absolutely alluring. In fact, he never really had to say much to them. At bars, women would slip past me to try to get to him, which was a new experience. Even my own mother thought he was beautiful and always asked about him.

Casey had apparently always attracted girls, even as a little boy. My best guess is that he exuded some secret-sauce pheromones that excite ancient female olfactory sensors. I can confirm that he carried an extra strong personal scent that filled the entire apartment and sometimes even clung to my own clothing.

Unlike me, a lone-wolf script analyst and freelance educator, Casey worked with celebrities. His boss Jonathan knew all the big famous names, and I heard the stories about them when Casey came home at night. Sharon Osbourne was easy to work with. Rob Lowe was terrific as well. But Rob's wife Sheryl was apparently monstrous. Once she asked Casey to fetch her tampons from the glove box in her Porsche.

"I'm gonna kill that woman," he told me. "I literally want to murder her."

His boss Jonathan didn't understand boundaries, like most people in Hollywood. So he worked Casey to the bone. When he wasn't planning installations, Casey was asked to socialize at West Hollywood restaurants and bars. I was invited to join them for dinner at a South African restaurant once, where I firsthand saw the iron fist in the velvet glove. Jonathan's manners were impeccable, but his understanding of personal limits was close to zero.

Once, at ten o'clock on a Tuesday night, Casey called me.

"Hey," he said, slurring his words.

"What's up?"

"So, um, I need you to pick me up—"

"Where are you?" I replied. I was in for the night. I'd already showered and lit a candle and poured myself a drink. I was wearing a turquoise robe and slippers.

"I'm at ..." he trailed off.

"Repeat that please."

"Rage!" he finally remembered. "I'm at Rage!"

At the time, that was the most famous gay nightclub in West Hollywood. It had even been a punchline in a joke uttered by Sam Rockwell in the movie *Matchstick Men*.

"Why are you at Rage?" I said, laughing.

"Can you just come pick me up?" His voice sounded like he was about to die.

"Fine. Meet me outside in ten minutes." I blew out the candle, put my drink in the refrigerator. Then, still wearing my bathrobe and slippers, I went downstairs and got in my red Ford pickup truck and drove over to Santa Monica Boulevard. I pulled up to the club, put my hazard lights on, and stepped out onto the sidewalk.

I stood there, in my robe and slippers. Astonished faces stared at me from the sidewalk. But I wasn't going inside that club. I just waited.

Finally Casey came stumbling out past the bouncers, wearing his business clothes. The booze on his breath was strong enough to peel the paint off my truck. It turned out that, at Jonathan's request, he'd spent the night with potential clients, slamming martinis on an empty stomach while cheering on men who were dancing nude in suspended cages. He barely made it home before throwing up.

That's commitment to your job.

He and Jonathan had quite a codependent dance going. Casey tried to quit the job twice, but Jonathan lured him back both times.

At last Casey escaped, finding a new position as the manager of a mid-century modern furniture store on La Brea Avenue. It was gorgeous stuff, and he loved running the store for a few years. You can see some of his furniture in the Christopher Nolan movie *Inception*. Remember the final shot of the film, with the top spinning endlessly on a long wooden table as Leo DiCaprio looks at the girls playing on the lawn? That was his company's table. It was their floor model. Casey himself loaned that table to Warner Brothers for five hundred dollars per day, and it's the one you see in the film. The studio ended up buying it.

We became fast friends. As a born-and-bred Californ-
ian, Casey had gone to Pepperdine University in Malibu
and had already lived in Los Angeles for almost a decade.
So he taught me about the city in ways that my other trans-
plant friends couldn't. He also slept with a wide range of
different women. I never knew who was coming out of his
bedroom on a Saturday morning. One that stuck around a
while, Rachel, had been Ben Stiller's assistant. She was a bit
crazy. I learned from her that Ben's problems had zilch to do
with fame and everything to do with his obsessive-compul-
sive disorder, which he struggled to manage. Half her job,
she said, was to keep a bottle of peach Snapple in Ben's
sightline at all times, or else he'd go into conniptions.

Our mutual trust was cemented by some automobile
issues. First came an accident: a 19-year-old tourist girl
visiting from Israel turned left and smashed into the front
end of my truck at the intersection of Sunset and Vine.
Casey was sitting next to me. The airbags blew up instantly,
causing contusions on his face and chin. Casey declined
medical help, or even to get upset. He just wore Band-Aids
on his face for the next few days.

Insurance declared my vehicle totaled, and I used the
payout to buy half of a new blue Ford Escape.

A year later, we decided to make a sweet little exchange.
Casey had a lemon of an Audi that he was trying to ditch. I
had about nine thousand dollars left to pay on the blue Ford
Escape. Meanwhile, I saw a Labor Day sales event at a local
dealership on the new Ford Escape Hybrid. That was the
vehicle I *really* wanted—the one with the huge battery in
the back, the sleeve around the brake pads that captured
heat energy and stored it as electric energy, the one that got
36 mpg. I was all about the hybrids when they first
came out.

So we struck a deal. Casey would pay the nine thousand dollars remaining on my blue Escape, I would pass ownership to him for a symbolic dollar, and then I would buy the new Escape Hybrid for myself. He loved the idea. We executed the entire plan in a single weekend. For the rest of our time as roommates, we had matching Ford Escapes, one gas, one hybrid, side by side in our parking spaces beneath our unit.

In a huge metropolis far from home, it was good to have someone I could trust.

———

CASEY ASKED me one day if I'd be interested in going to see his family's home in Santa Ynez. That's up in central California, in the hills of wine country, past Santa Barbara. He'd grown up there and he wanted to show me the area.

Sure. Why not?

I wasn't prepared for what I found. His family's house was a sprawling glass mid-century box on a hilltop, at least five thousand square feet. Panoramic views presented themselves out of every floor-to-ceiling glass window in the home. The sounds of horses and cattle sounded from the neighbors' estates. Bo Derek lived next door, and the famous Reagan ranch was visible in the hills on the other side of the valley.

Casey had grown up *wealthy*. I didn't know that. He'd never mentioned it.

His father was a retired radiologist who'd attended both USC and Yale Medical School. Dr. Carter was a stiff, stern, exacting man, a former Mormon. Over a glass of a local cabernet sauvignon, we found that we enjoyed each other's company—a lot. His dad was exactly forty years and one day older than me, and he found my big mouth amusing.

Politically, we were at sixes and sevens. He was a life-long Republican, the type that wants to be left alone, who looks down on the human race like a puppy that'd just piddled the carpet. Me, I was raised by Midwestern Polish Catholics, some of whom were union Democrats. I worried about things like the tragedy of the commons, which baffled him. He and I jousted quite a bit over cigars in his hot tub that first night, with Casey acting as referee.

I came back for more visits, and I grew even closer with Dr. Carter. I didn't realize it, but later that would spell the end of my friendship with his son.

———

AFTER FOUR YEARS TOGETHER, I moved out of that apartment and in with my fiancée, Fang. You can read about her coming up.

That meant the end of our roommate relationship, but I asked Casey to be the best man at my wedding a year later. He agreed, and we got some great photos. It felt good to know I could still rely on a male friend, particularly after my experience with Brian's descent into self-hatred.

Then he changed.

Like Brian, Casey grew weird, distant, preoccupied. I remember how he grew physically uncomfortable while I was telling him about an idea I'd had for a book series about a female gemstone detective who goes on adventurous investigative assignments in foreign countries. (A few months later, I began publishing the Ainsley Walker Gemstone Travel Mystery series, which you can purchase wherever books are sold.)

His phone calls dried up. His text messages stopped. I was newly married and busy with my own disaster of a spouse, but his silence was noticeable.

Finally, I sent him a short email asking essentially, what was up. He replied the next day, explaining how busy he'd been.

Then, in the next paragraph, he shoved the head of our friendship into the guillotine and dropped the blade.

Here's a portion of the email—

Due to all this I truly haven't had time to hang out as much as I used to, with you or others. There's just too much to do. I also, unfortunately, have been feeling a bit uncomfortable. It's nothing specific to call out, I think you and I get along fine, but I don't really connect on a level that is sustainable. It's been a while since I've felt this and I was finding it harder to feel comfortable when we hung out. As much time as we have spent together, it has felt rather superficial (not a negative, lots of friends are superficial, but it just isn't something to build on in a serious way). Eventually it began to fizzle out and feel a bit forced, and I became less and less relaxed.

I think we were good friends and had a lot of fun, and it was a ball, but it's time for me to move along.

I found that I was thinking less about us doing things and not finding the urgency to call, which I'm sure you noticed here and there last year. So, it seemed an appropriate time to begin distancing. I initiated less, and found that I was more comfortable with the space, and continued moving back. When I noticed I was happier on my own, I found the only way to really handle this was to end it completely.

This depressed me for a good long while.

I had rotten luck keeping male friends as an adult. I mean, Casey had been the best man at my wedding two years earlier—then decided that he couldn't stand my presence. I was friend-dumped for mysterious reasons known only to his mysterious psyche.

But were those reasons really that mysterious?

———

I'D LONG NOTICED that Casey had zero male friends, other than me. All of his relationships tended to be with women, and those didn't last long either. He'd always found reasons to break up with every girl he'd ever dated, and they didn't have to be legit reasons. The excuses ranged from *she tasted like Pepsi* to *she ordered chicken too often.*

Back then, I just thought he was squirmy and weird with relationships. Today, I know what to call him: an avoidant attachment style.

On top of that, he and his father had never seen eye to eye. Dr. Carter was a fault-finding intellectual with an eagle eye for error. Nothing passed across his field of vision without being analyzed and criticized. As a result, Casey had always carried the feeling that he could never live up to his father's scrutiny. Around his father, he grew passive and sometimes seemed to physically wilt.

Enter me—excitedly sweeping into his family's house, dazzling his parents with witty conversation, creating a fast connection with the same man who'd made him feel like a worm for so long. In fact, for the last two years, Dr. Carter had even started inviting me to visit his home without Casey. So I did that, several times, which made the situation worse. Seeing me win his father's approval must've felt unbearable.

Looking back, I could have pulled back on those visits, just out of deference to my friend. But he never spelled out any of his issues to me, other than his strange refusal to use the words *dad* or *father*. He always called his father by his full name, Edward Carter. He left it up to me to play psychological detective and piece all this together after the fact.

But it wouldn't have mattered. Casey' dissatisfaction with me, himself, and life was deep enough that he soon fled California completely. A few months after sending that email to me, he literally sold all his things and moved to Hawaii.

Word on the street said that he shipped over the blue Ford Escape that I'd sold to him years earlier. He apparently found a new job in furniture somewhere in Oahu. And he has lived there for the last thirteen years, geographically as far away as he can get from his own father without leaving the United States.

Soon after that, Dr. Carter stopped inviting me to his house. I think the world of their family and wish all of them well. But I also wish that things had turned out differently.

9
CATALINA

Southern California is packed with barely functional head cases. *Tip the world over on its side,* said architect Frank Lloyd Wright, *and everything loose will land in Los Angeles.* It makes dating there a real chore. Everybody's got a relationship horror story.

Age twenty-six is when guys start to get cuffed by baby-minded women feeling the pressure of too many lost uterine linings. It's the age when many of us begin to turn our eyes towards mortgages, promotions, a full night's sleep. It's the age when a large number of eligible men find themselves yanked off the dating market and cajoled down the wedding aisle.

But none of that happened to me at age twenty-six.

Instead, I met Catalina.

She worked at the office where I read scripts. Catalina had short black hair and big brown eyes and a large toothy smile. She also had a photogenic face, a bit like Marilyn Monroe.

Like that famous woman, Catalina suffered from

borderline personality disorder. But I didn't know that right away.

I started messaging her on a primitive messaging service —AOL, I think. I flirted and cajoled and begged her to come out with me. At some point, she caved in, and we embarked on a crazy summer together.

My roommate at the time, Noah, was skeptical. He was exactly the type of best-friend character in a movie who cocks his head and asks the protagonist: *Are you sure you know what you're doing?*

Of course I did. (Narrator voice: He didn't.)

———

AT AGE THIRTY-ONE, Catalina was five years older than me, and her behavior was extreme. She'd been through a weird string of huge professional ambitions, followed by quick collapse of those same ambitions. At one time, she'd fully decided to become a film director, until about a month later, when it dawned on her that she'd never be as successful as Steven Spielberg. So she immediately gave up. She'd once impulsively shaved her head totally bald. Another time, I watched her leap off a roof into a swimming pool, that famous party stunt you see in movies that can go so horribly wrong.

Mostly, she was directionless.

It turned out that she was seeing a therapist who'd recommended to her that she not date anybody, because she wasn't emotionally stable enough. The therapist had urged her to start baking as a way of grounding herself during episodes of dissociation.

Catalina started ridiculous fights with me, fights that

wouldn't end until I removed myself from her presence. Most of those spats began on the flimsiest of offenses, or on straw men, or on figments of her imagination, or on nothing at all. Once, at a social event on the Sunset Strip, I was chatting with a female attorney when Catalina grabbed me and pulled me out to the sidewalk and yelled at me for my enormous insensitivity. Then she began convulsing at the waist: she was suffering a panic attack, triggered by the sight of me speaking to another woman. She pulled a tab of Xanax from her purse and swallowed it. I drove her home and put her to bed.

At other times, she'd suddenly decide to break up, claiming that she didn't want to become a Midwestern housewife. I don't know where that claim originated from. At the time, I didn't want to return to the Midwest, and I didn't want that from her. But the made-up version of me that existed only inside her crazy skull evidently was making a lot of racket. I shouldn't have taken her seriously, but I did anyways, charging forward with my spear of logic into her viper's nest of irrationality. It did no good whatsoever. She was just like a maze, as John Mayer sang, all the walls continually changing.

After the breakups, Catalina would change her mind again, and come over to my apartment with a tray of cupcakes as an apology. I'd bite my tongue to stop from pointing out that baking cupcakes is a very Midwestern housewife thing to do.

My roommate Noah loved the apology cupcakes. "She's crazy," he said, wiping his mouth with a napkin, "but she knows how to bake."

Some of my exchanges with her were done on messenger, so I had written proof of her insanity. I showed the conversations to Andy once. He was quite sensitive towards women, but Catalina pushed him to the breaking point.

"This is a great example of how insane a woman can be," he said bluntly, pointing at the screen. "You could save these and use them in a scene."

I listened to the advice and did save those conversations for many years. But several laptop changes later, the file has sadly been lost.

Catalina introduced me to some interesting people though, and if I'm being honest, those connections were one of the reasons I stayed with her for half a year. She'd found a new job as assistant to Mike Tollin, the well-known Hollywood power player who executive produced *Smallville* and, more recently, *The Last Dance* documentary about Michael Jordan and the Chicago Bulls.

One day, Tollin asked Catalina if I played basketball: he kept a weekly game running in his backyard court on Saturday mornings and was looking for some fresh players. I'm decent at hoops and agreed to play. For a few weeks, I went over every weekend. Once, I ended up guarding Kel Mitchell, the star of *Kenan & Kel*, a popular Nickelodeon show that Tollin also executive produced.

On another occasion, Catalina invited me out to dinner in Los Feliz with a friend of a friend named Marty, plus some others. That's all she told me about him. We drove to Marty's house; he was a sixtyish man in a handsome English sport coat. He announced that all six of us would leave together to the restaurant in his car, which turned out to be a brand-new white Rolls-Royce with cream leather interior.

Who was this guy?

Over margaritas and taco plates at Mexico City, a now-closed landmark restaurant in the neighborhood, I found out that Marty's full name was Marty Krofft. Together with his older brother Sid, they had produced several popular children's television puppet shows of the 1960s and 1970s such as *H.R. Pufnstuf, Land of the Lost*, and *Sigmund and the Sea Monsters*. All those psychedelic titles predated me, but I chatted with Marty for close to half an hour that night. That man couldn't have been nicer or more respectful to all of us young bucks. He's gone now, but I know I'm not the only one who remembers him fondly.

Catalina and I did share a love for camping. I loved getting dirty and sleeping on the hard ground for a couple nights at a time. California has all types of deserts, mountains, forests, and oceans, and we scrammed out of the city every weekend we could get. We explored north of Lake Isabella along the Kern River, hiking the Whiskey Flat Trail to natural waterslides in the rocks. We headed up to Bishop, roaming the scenic and spooky Bodie State Park, an immaculately preserved Old West ghost town. On the border with Nevada, we drove up the White Mountains to the ancient bristlecone pine forest, which contains the oldest tree in existence: the five-thousand-year-old Methuselah, whose identity remains a secret.

One weekend I rode with Catalina to meet her family in Modesto, California. Her father was a retired school administrator, the son of penniless Mexican immigrants. Her mother had been one of his middle school students when he was a young twentysomething teacher. They said they'd waited to start dating until she'd turned eighteen. At that point, they'd been married 35 years, so they must've known something that other people didn't. I won't pass judgment. He made guacamole so good that I would sell my own internal organs to get another spoonful of it.

Her mother displayed weird behaviors. She flew off the handle a fair amount that weekend. She made strange pronouncements and tossed them into the middle of the room, where they landed with a thud like a dead fish. She also sprayed my laptop with a garden hose and didn't seem to care that she'd nearly ruined all my professional and personal files. She had another daughter too, Alicia, who lived in Miami. Alicia worked as a personal trainer and had bought herself huge breast implants a few years earlier. I gathered that she was troubled, like her sister.

Overall, none of them were my usual vibe, including Catalina.

———

THE END of the relationship occurred in the most Hollywood way possible. Catalina was asked to accompany her boss to South Carolina, where he was scheduled to direct a movie. Titled *Radio*, it starred Ed Harris and Cuba Gooding Jr. as a high school football coach and a developmentally disabled young man. You may have seen the film. More likely, you haven't.

I was a bowl of mixed feelings. I couldn't stand her anymore, but I wasn't ready for her to leave either. It was the only time in my life that I'd felt so confused.

"I have to go," she said. "It's a great opportunity."

"It really is," I replied. "Should we stay together, or should we just end it?"

"Well, I've always said distance makes the heart go wander," she said.

That wasn't a yes or a no. It was a threat of infidelity. She was scheduled to leave for three months, starting in September. We'd only been dating since April. I decided to let her go and begin dating other people. Finding another woman wasn't an easy task for me at the time. I was a young nobody.

Catalina sublet her apartment to a twenty-year-old actor, and to be nice, I promised to check up on her stuff now and then to make sure he wasn't selling it for drugs. On the day of her flight, I drove her to LAX and said goodbye.

Then, back in my car, I sat behind the steering wheel and cried.

This was way out of character. I almost never cry. In fact, I've only cried three times in my adult life. The other two were while summiting the highest peak in the U.S., and later when my father was diagnosed with cancer. So this chick had really wormed her way into my psyche.

Almost immediately, she began calling me from across the country. Once every day or two, usually at night, always asking what I'd been doing. We were in the weird gray space where commitment was a pipe dream, but a total breakup wasn't yet possible.

After a few weeks, she asked if I would fly out to see her. I reluctantly agreed. Part of the attraction, I admit, was the chance to visit a feature film set. It'd been on my bucket list. We settled on my birthday week, which is in November.

———

I ARRIVED in the tiny rural town of Walterboro, South Carolina, which had been taken over by the film production company. It was trapped in time, with soda fountains and other small-town paraphernalia long gone from modern life.

The townspeople were thrilled. Having a movie in their lil' ole neck of the woods was the most exciting thing they'd seen in decades. As I was buying a coffee at a local drug store, I looked up to see the cashier pointing a disposable camera at me. *Click.* She'd snapped my photo.

"What was that for?" I said.

"Oh no reason."

"I'm not an actor. I'm just visiting set for a few days."

She put the camera away. "Well, that don't matter. I'm taking pictures of everybody coming through here. You never know!"

My first night, Catalina took me on set for a big scene. They were filming a Christmas tree lighting in the downtown city square. There were about a hundred extras milling around behind a chain link fence.

"Do you want to be one of them?" said Catalina. "We can make you a key extra."

That meant the camera would linger on me. Ugh. I'm allergic to performing in front of a lens.

"No thanks," I said. "It looks like they're in a concentration camp. I'll just sit over here and pretend I'm directing."

I sat down in one of those tall Hollywood director's chairs, right behind her boss, the actual director. Mike was waiting for his crew to set up the shot, so I made a crack about Philadelphia sports teams, just loud enough for him to hear. It caught his ear, and he turned around and briefly defended the Phillies before returning to work.

One person who looked less than thrilled to see me was Ed Harris, the actor. I understand he likes to keep a controlled set, in order to maintain his focus, and here was this unfamiliar young man lounging near the camera, bantering with passersby. Harris is an intimidating dude, even more in real life than onscreen, and his intense blue eyes were boring into mine. He seemed to be weighing whether to boot me, so I stopped talking, grabbed Catalina, and put my arm around her. That seemed to reassure him, and I was silently allowed to stay.

Quickly I learned that the old saying is true: movie sets

are boring. After a couple of hours, I grew tired of sitting around. Over hot chocolate at a nearby cafe, I talked screenplays with Cuba Gooding Jr.'s producing partner. A black man, he cracked jokes about the hundreds of "first black" scripts he'd received after Cuba had won an Oscar a few years earlier. Then I tried chatting with a United Talent Agency agent, Jeremy Zimmer, who'd flown out for the weekend. He was such a caricature it nearly made my eyes bleed. A fast-talking Hollywood creature in a sleek suit navigating a small Southern town, a mobile phone pressed to his ear. He was pure comedy.

Finally the filming started, with Ed and Cuba (wearing fake teeth) in 1970s period clothing. They hung a Christmas ornament on a tree while people stood around applauding. Watch the movie, and you'll see the scene.

A few takes, and it was all over. Catalina and I were walking off the set, towards the police barricades and the crowds down the street, when someone tackled me from behind. I found myself in a huge hug against my will. When I disengaged myself, I found that my assailant was Cuba Gooding, Jr. He was still wearing his fake teeth and period clothing and had remained in his developmentally disabled character. Then he threw himself on Catalina, squeezed her, giggled, and skipped away.

They call that method acting. I don't think he left character during the shoot.

The next day we went back on set, and this time Catalina introduced me to some of the crew. A sound guy named Tim nodded at me, then quickly went back to work. A set design guy regaled me with anecdotes about working on the movie *Se7en* under the famously demanding David Fincher. Later, I dawdled around craft services, eating free meals.

The next day, Catalina and I went to Savannah for my birthday, and something felt off. Finally, it came time for me to leave on Monday, and things felt even more off.

A few days after I got home, Catalina called to dump me. We were finished, she said. She informed me that she'd found a new guy, that she was serious about him, and that I was last week's news, literally.

"Who's the new guy?" I asked.

"Tim," she said.

"The sound guy?" I asked.

"Yeah."

Now I understood why he'd avoided talking to me. In fact, it was ridiculous of her to introduce us at all.

"Why did you ask me to come out to visit you?" I asked.

"I don't know," she said. "It wasn't serious between me and him when you bought the ticket. But now it is."

I don't remember anything else except hanging up the phone. I felt sick to my stomach.

The clichés are real, and they happen all the time. People in Hollywood fall in love on movie sets. They're susceptible to flights of romance, which happen more on movie sets than at ordinary jobs.

Still, I felt relieved that my six-month horror story of a relationship was over and done.

———

But Catalina's bizarre life story rolled on. Because I stayed in touch with a lot of mutuals, I heard all the updates, and it wasn't pretty.

That breakup phone call had occurred on November 15. By Christmas, they told me that Catalina was pregnant. It wasn't mine, I knew that much.

"Just don't get knocked up," a mutual friend, Angus Oblong, complained to me when delivering the news. "That was *all* I asked her to do. And she went and did it anyways. God, this sucks!"

His name hasn't been changed, and you may distantly recognize it. Angus is an animator who had a television program on the WB, *The Oblongs*, for one season way back in 2001. He hasn't done much else in the decades since, except sell bizarre drawings from his website. He likes to attend comic cons wearing white facepaint with a red clown nose.

Catalina married Tim the sound guy a few months later. She gave birth to their boy a few months after that.

"Hey," said Angus' partner to me one day, "guess who came to our roller-skating party last week?"

"I can't imagine who," I said.

"Yeah, she acted like a bitch and ruined it," he said. "I thought you might want to know."

"I do appreciate that."

We pounded fists.

———

Two YEARS LATER, another mutual friend, Maureen, asked to meet me for a drink. She and I had always gotten along well. Maureen was an occasional actress, but more often a wry observer of the entertainment industry. She loved my impersonation of Alan Rickman, who played Severus Snape in the Harry Potter movies. By her request, I used to leave messages for her in character. Imagine Rickman's distinctive voice: *Hello Maureen, this is Alan—I've done Othello, I've done Chekhov, and now I'm doing your voicemail.*

"Hey, so I have news," she said. "Catalina's sister died."

I'd never met her sister. "Oh yeah? How did that happen?"

"She drank herself to death in her own bed."

If true, it wouldn't have surprised me. The family had mental illness. According to the obituary that I later read, Alicia had been only 31 years old.

"That's too bad."

"And something else. Catalina's leaving California."

"Where to?"

"She and her husband are moving to Michigan."

Picture me doing that squeak-squeak circular rubbing motion with my fists over my eye sockets. "I'm sorry, did you say Michigan?"

"Yeah."

"That's my state! That's where I'm from." I felt suddenly defensive.

"They're moving to, what's it called, Traverse City? I guess that's where he grew up. They had a second kid too."

My mind floated backwards in time, to all her jousting against an imaginary version of me who was asking her to become a Midwestern housewife. Now here she was, becoming a Midwestern housewife, the role that she so fiercely had fought against, for another man.

I concluded that she'd been seriously projecting. Part of her had wanted to leave Los Angeles and live a quiet life as a housewife in flyover country. But this was an unacceptable urge, I guess, so she'd been pushing those thoughts onto me in order to fight them.

———

It turns out that Catalina and Tim the sound guy made a good match. They've stayed married for over twenty years, as of this writing. I can't fault that, but I have no idea how she's managed to not destroy her family. When I knew her, she couldn't keep a goldfish alive.

Catalina remained a Midwestern housewife for almost a decade before the family decided to return to Los Angeles. Her husband continues to work in sound, on a lot of big-name television series and movies that you've probably seen. I think he may have won an Oscar, but I don't care enough to check.

I truly don't know how anybody could stay married to borderline personality disorder for that long. At first I thought Tim must be deaf and couldn't hear her crazy rantings, but then I remembered that he works in sound recording. Maybe he has the patience of a saint. Or maybe motherhood has stabilized her personality. Maybe she found a new, more effective therapist. It could be a combination of things.

The experience taught me a lot about borderline personality syndrome. I hadn't even known what it was prior to meeting her. On a recommendation, after the breakup, I read *Stop Walking On Eggshells*, by Randi Kreger, which helped me understand the depth of the problem. I learned what Cluster-B type personalities were. I promised not to ever open myself up to one again.

But then I did, a few years later. And the next one was even worse, because I married her.

FANG: THE LOVE-BOMBING BEGINS

Picture it: Tall, sexy, legs up to her neck, an apple bottom that swung a bit too much when she walked in her designer jeans. Twenty-four-year-old southern California girl with a big mane of blonde hair. She had a swagger, like she knew that everybody was looking at her.

She was right. They were.

On our first date, another guy tried hitting on her the moment I left to the bathroom. I couldn't blame him.

Second date, third date, fourth date. I tumbled into love with her, even though I preferred brunettes. Still, who was I to complain about this gift that had fallen into my lap? She had college degrees in creative writing and art history. She was funny too, literally making me laugh out loud.

Today, I understand the humor was an expression of her aggression. But I didn't know that then.

She worked part-time at Cedars-Sinai Medical Center, near my apartment. So we saw each other a couple times a week, at lunchtime. We spent all our weekends together. After a few weeks, she said we ought to be exclusive. I quickly agreed. In my mind, it was never going to get better than this. I felt happy. After almost a decade of dating—I was turning thirty shortly—the world felt reborn.

After a month together, she went home to visit her parents in San Diego. *I'm going to marry this guy*, she told them. I found this out years later.

We became inseparable. She was very emotional, as highly reactive as an Australian shepherd. This was not my usual cup of tea, but I decided to strap myself to the rocket anyways. I was entranced by her personality, her body, her humor, everything.

Halloween came. I dressed as the odious Hugh Hefner, she a Playboy bunny. Bustier, fishnets, heels, pink ears. Out on the streets of West Hollywood that night, we drew a thousand stares. They were all looking at her.

We even bought plane tickets for a journey to South America. Two weeks, no tour guide, just us and our combined Spanish careening around Argentina and Uruguay. We barely had the money to afford it, but who cared. It felt like the world was our oyster. Photos from that trip still pluck a heartstring.

I know your next question. If she's your ex-wife, weren't there warnings signs?

Of course there were.

11

FANG: THE RED FLAGS

I didn't overlook her issues, though some of them had been hidden. Of the ones I could see, I just assumed, in my infinite wisdom, that they didn't apply to me. If I didn't want them to matter, they wouldn't matter.

Overconfidence: the Achilles' heel of the young successful white male.

Those red flags, in no particular order—

- The **tramp stamp** on her lower back. It was a classic tell. I knew what it usually meant, and I know what it usually means now. I just didn't care.
- The **screaming fits** when her desires couldn't be fulfilled. On one occasion, I had to hold the phone away from my ear, the bellowing grew so loud. I explained them to myself in a few ways. *It's a phase. She's five years younger than me. She'll grow out of it.* (Narrator voice: *She didn't.*)

- Her closet crammed full of **designer shoes** and **designer clothing**. On a part-time fifteen-dollar-an-hour wage.
- The **Sex and the City ringtone** on her phone. That song haunts me to this day.
- **The way she always walked half a step ahead of me.** If I sped up, she sped up too. She refused to let me lead.

I justified all those warnings to myself in the following ways:

- **Her parents had a strong marriage.** High school sweethearts, fun people, crazy but loving.
- **Her parents liked me.** But her father was a handful. The first night I met him, he got so drunk that he burned his own couch on his driveway. Months later, in Hawaii, I went around finishing other people's cocktails in a tiki bar, at which point he told me he loved me. Honestly, I grew to love him too, like everybody did. He was the life of the party, an absolute force of nature. The type of person that they will tell stories about for decades after he passes. You may know the type.
- **I had total confidence in my ability to overcome anything through the force of my own will.** This was my biggest mistake. Some people can't be controlled.
- **She was smart.** I assumed I could reason with a smart person. But you know what they say about assumptions.

I don't remember how it happened in my head, but after a year and a half of this rapturous love affair, I decided it was time that we get married. I searched for and found a travel package—only one thousand dollars for a winter trip for two to Rome, Italy, including plane and hotel. Fang had always wanted to go there, had even studied Italian for three years.

I suggested the vacation. She gave an enthusiastic thumbs up. I purchased it, then gave her a card a day later. Inside I wrote: *Do you know what's going to happen in Rome?* As she read it, I held her eyes.

"What's going to happen?" she said.

"Let's go shopping this Saturday," I replied.

She grew excited. "For what?"

"You know for what," I said.

Her eyes lit up. She went running around like a beautiful but overstimulated rat. That Saturday, with her at my side, I bought the eight-thousand-dollar ring of her dreams, on credit, from an Armenian jeweler in the downtown Los Angeles jewelry district. That was six weeks' salary, more or less, at that time. I followed the classic advice for chumps, not knowing any better.

You may have noticed that I was the driver of the engagement and the marriage, not her. This isn't typical. I guess it showed how certain I was that we were meant to be together.

We flew to Rome. I proposed, she accepted. We walked and ate, walked and ate. We walked so much that the soles of my boots collapsed.

When we touched down again in Los Angeles, she had a ring on her finger and I had stars in my eyes. To outsiders, I'd just landed a prize—a smart and leggy California blonde in her mid-twenties. We were happy. We were starting to plan our lives together.

But I had little idea of the shitshow that I'd just invited into my life.

12

FANG: IT GROWS WORSE

Nighttime in Seville, Spain. The smell of jacaranda floating in the air. The sound of flamenco singers wafting out of windows.

I watched Fang stalk ahead of me down the cobblestone street, shouting something. Then I figured it out.

She was threatening to divorce me.

My crime was minimal, if it even existed. I most likely had disagreed with her about the angle of a seat at a table. It truly doesn't matter. This was the fifth day of our honeymoon, and the seventh day of our marriage. She'd already whipped out the "d" word.

I wish I was making this up, but I'm not.

It wasn't the last time either. There was no disagreement that she wouldn't escalate. Express a single skeptical comment that pricked at her perceived status, and I would find myself on an express elevator to an existential crisis in our marriage. She did it over and over and over.

Two months before the wedding, she grew especially hostile. She was like a feral cat backed into a corner. She'd been gung-ho to plan the wedding, and I knew that she'd told her mother early on that she knew I was the one. So this new fury was very bizarre.

I dragged her to two different marriage counselors to find out what was going on inside her head. One counselor indicated that he wanted to see her privately, which gave me relief. But she never went.

I considered canceling the wedding, but that would've meant the loss of tens of thousands of dollars. It would have inconvenienced many of my guests flying in from the Midwest. And I was confident that she could be brought under control.

Fang managed to calm down, and the wedding went on as planned. But after that, during the first year, she stated repeatedly that our marriage wasn't guaranteed to continue.

"Listen," I would say, "you and I are married so you'd better make the best of it."

"For now," she would reply.

That is one of the worst things you can say to a spouse. I viewed our relationship as permanent, but she viewed us as temporary. In her mind, there was already an asterisk next to the marriage.

It grew worse. This woman's narcissism was so vast that she couldn't let any past slights die. She dredged up the slimmest injury to her ego from the past and flung it back at me, repeatedly. She did this so often that I created a stock response:

Stop being negative about the past, and start being positive about the future.

I'd invited a kitten to live in my house. That kitten had grown into a tiger, and it wanted to be let out.

———

THE BEDROOM PROBLEMS began in the second or third year of marriage, when Fang's sex drive died.

Every year or so, Fang changed her birth control method. She hopped from one type of oral contraceptive pill to another, from an IUD to an injection, and finally to nothing at all. All these changes wreaked havoc on her hormones.

Many of the problems began when she went off the oral contraceptive pills. We managed to have sex maybe once a month at most, and every time was awful. She complained that it hurt (true). She complained that I didn't know how to touch her anymore (false). She complained that I had no sexual skills (very false).

"If I'm that inept," I asked her, "then why did you agree to marry me?"

She had no answer to that. It was all bullshit anyways. The truth was that she'd lost attraction, plain and simple. And she'd begun projecting all our problems onto me because she couldn't accept responsibility for her own changing hormonal profile.

There was one moment of honesty. One night, after a bad attempt at sexual intercourse, Fang started crying. She confessed that she was a bad wife. Through her tears, she told me to go and find another woman, that it wasn't fair to treat me like this.

"No," I replied, "I made a vow to you, and I'm going to keep it."

I was raised to be loyal, faithful, reliable, like my father. But that was a mistake with Fang. At that moment, I absolutely should have found another woman. But these are the things we only see in retrospect.

Since then, I've learned that birth control pills change

the type of man that a woman desires. As a result, a woman who finds and marries a man while taking oral contraceptives often finds her spouse less attractive after she stops taking them. This dynamic is responsible for the death of many young marriages. According to one study, women who stop taking oral contraceptive pills during their marriage are divorced at a nearly 50% higher rate than women who don't.

That's exactly what happened to me. Today I tell women to stay off birth control pills when they're looking for a husband. Join me in getting the word out.

————

IN THE SEVEN-PLUS years we were together, Fang went through five major job changes. She went from executive assistant at a hospital, to executive assistant at an artistic foundation, to assistant fashion buyer at major fashion chain, to salesperson at a shipping company, and finally to salesperson for a large ecommerce company.

I supported her in every one of the changes. But I soon recognized the same cycle of hire, excitement, disillusionment, and exit. She couldn't stay in any job for more than about nine months before she started casting around for the next opportunity. She was a job hopper.

To her, life was a game of catch and release.

She did the same with clothing. Even though Fang's closet was stuffed with 500 shirts, tops, pants, or dresses, and 90 pairs of expensive designer high heels, her shopping addiction didn't abate. In fact, it migrated online. Three or four days a week, I found another delivery box waiting in front of our door. Inside was another item of clothing that she would inspect, review, and usually return.

Catch and release.

Same with cats. Fang was constantly adopting cats, getting bored with them, and returning them to the shelter. In five years, there were at least eight cats that she cycled through the house. I'd never owned a cat before, and I just watched it all, perplexed.

Catch and release.

I started getting a different sense of her. My wife was either a borderline grifter or a dopamine addict constantly searching for the next hit. I haven't figured out which, even today. She'd sift through everything and anyone in search of the tiniest edge.

That included husbands.

———

TATTOOS PROVED to be another conflict.

I've never liked them. I can't explain why, and it makes me feel out of step with my own generation, which is covered in ink.

When we met, Fang had a single tramp stamp on her lower back. It was a dumb decision at age eighteen, and she regretted it. It caused a lot of smirks and raised eyebrows. But then she got a second tattoo, this one on her ankle, while out with a girlfriend one night. We weren't married yet, so I couldn't complain.

A year later, she came home with a third tattoo across her upper back and neck. I was furious. I didn't want to be married to a human billboard, and I told her this. She ignored my protests and said that she'd already made plans to get wrist tattoos next. She said that she'd already chosen the ancient runes.

I told her that I didn't want to married to a person

covered in tattoos.

Evidently it worked, because a couple years passed without a peep about ink from her.

Then, a few months before she walked out, she came home one day with plastic wrap around both her wrists. She'd gone ahead and gotten huge wrist tats of weird symbols meant to symbolize her ancestors. Nobody understood any of it, not even her parents.

My wishes had been steamrolled. I was irrelevant.

————

MOCKERY, belittling, derision—all the building blocks of a healthy, respectful relationship, right?

She displayed all of them.

The maid-of-honor at our wedding once told me that Fang was a man-hater. I didn't see it at first—she was hiding it from me during the engagement—but once we were married, it came out in force.

She began lashing me with her sharp mouth, reducing my masculinity at every turn rather than supporting it. She made fun of my work, of my income, of my clothes, of my walk, of my yoga exercises. Her stabs were so incessant that I found myself getting physically sick more often than ever, usually an upper-respiratory infection four times a year. That, in turn, made her mock me even further.

Years later, I learned that a toxic spouse often depresses a person's immune system, causing increased illnesses and infections.

Regardless, I don't let people push me around, so I defended myself. In the face of her aggression, I'd say, *When are you going to respect me? Give me a day and a time so I can come back then.* She never physically abused me, other than slapping my shoulder a bit too hard. But verbal abuse is a different story.

One Christmas Eve, we were driving down to her family's house in San Diego when I made an innocuous comment about wanting to visit New York again. It'd been years since I'd been there. Fang, who was driving the vehicle—she refused to let anybody drive her car, including me—had already drunk a glass or two of red wine earlier that night and decided to escalate that single comment into an apocalyptic argument packed with misinterpretations and straw men. She began screaming at me, and I yelled back. We were on I-5, somewhere around Camp Pendleton, and she soon was swerving like a madwoman. I sensed that she was dangerously out of control and suggested that she pull over, mostly so I could talk her down.

She pulled off the freeway and parked in an empty patch of gravel. I tried to talk sense to her, but there was a bizarre insanity in her eyes. It might have been a psychotic break. My words were useless against it, tiny little arrows bouncing off a dragon's armor. It was the one time that I feared for my safety. She was that deranged.

I told her that her behavior was making me afraid for my own safety. I told her that she could continue onto her parents' house, but that I would not be riding any further in the vehicle with her. Then I stepped out. She tore away.

I was alone on Christmas Eve. There was nothing nearby, anywhere. I began calculating how to get to the nearest Amtrak station so that I could catch a train back to Los Angeles in the morning. I wondered if the Marines would help me out, if I could find any. It was past midnight by now, so technically it was Christmas Day.

Fifteen minutes later, she came roaring back down the deserted road. Evidently she had a change of heart. I think she realized that she wouldn't know how to explain my absence to her parents. Money and loss of perceived status were the only incentives that she ever really listened to. She briefly apologized and asked me to come back inside the car. I hesitantly agreed. We didn't say a word for the next hour until our arrival at her parents' house.

A lot of these conflicts were rooted in her disrespect and distrust of men. It was a deep damage caused by events that occurred in her extended family when she was young. In the span of three years during her early adolescence—

- Her 80-year-old grandfather had left her grandmother after a lifetime of his blatant infidelity.
- A close family member had been sexually molested by his athletic coach.
- Her father, a self-destructive and emotionally neglected party boy, had broken his own back when he drove into an open mine shaft on a motorbike at age 42, putting him in traction for six months.

Developmentally speaking, early adolescence is a delicate time for girls. The lesson that Fang absorbed from all these events was simple: men were not to be trusted.

———

WATER SEEKS ITS OWN LEVEL, and Fang kept a circle of screwed-up girlfriends too.

She gravitated to drama queens with emotional

dysfunction because they filled her own need for constant stimulation. Some of the women were sleazy. Some were working through their own trauma. Some were serial cheaters. Some were abusive control freaks. Some were mentally ill.

I barred one, Michelle, from ever entering my home again because of the abusive way she treated her boyfriend, Landon, the final time they'd visited. I'd seen them act that way in public too, and I decided to draw a line in the sand. To my surprise, Fang agreed with me.

A decade earlier, Michelle had moved from Indiana to Los Angeles to—surprise!—pursue acting. It hadn't worked out. She had a smart mind and was very organized, but her emotional damage was evident. Most of her trauma was directed at Landon, who she alternately abused and controlled. She scheduled all his weekend activities on a clipboard, which she sarcastically called the clipboard of fun. He had zero say in both the relationship and his own life. Seeking male camaraderie, I'd tried to make friends with him, separate from our two difficult women. But his self-esteem was so low, and his social anxiety disorder so crippling, that we couldn't connect. I gave up. He was doomed to stay an NPC.

A second girlfriend, Maria, told me upon meeting, "I will fuck you up if you do anything to hurt her." Classic—I was presumed guilty of misogyny and abuse without uttering more than two words. Incidentally, Maria had fucked every single firefighter at her local fire station. She was the village water tank: everyone had had a pump.

A third one, Jessica, had been banned from at least one hotel for public drunkenness and verbal assault. She was a borderline personality with several legal actions in process against her.

A fourth one, Carolyn, was an attorney whose own father was serving a prison sentence for violent crime. I never found out the whole story about that. Still, Carolyn was the only person I'd met who could disappear in front of your eyes. She dissociated so completely from conversations that it was like she wasn't there.

They say that you are the average of the four people you spend the most time with. By that metric, Fang was a very screwed-up individual.

———

EARLY IN OUR RELATIONSHIP, Fang was earning $15 an hour. I was making double that, with a lot more hours, so I supported our lives to an extent. I paid for most entertainment. I paid the rent for the five years we lived together.

That was good, because she was drowning in credit card debt. My memory is dim, but I believe she had nearly fifty thousand dollars of it. Those designer heels hadn't paid for themselves, and Fang's shopping addiction was impacting every part of her life.

To help her, I took $15,000 of credit card debt off her hands and transferred it onto one of my own cards. Slowly, I began to pay it off. Over time, including interest, I paid over $20,000 on that alone. When she started making more money than me, I expected that she would return the favor in some way.

Nope.

That was the precise moment that she walked out on me. She didn't see things the same way I did—you know, in terms of fairness, or reciprocity, or double-entry bookkeeping. Her attitude was *See ya, sucka*!

Divorce court didn't do me wrong. Instead, I did the

damage to myself, by exposing myself financially to a person who took advantage of my willingness to help her.

———

LIKE MOST WOMEN, Fang did make it known that she wanted to buy a house at some point. Soon she began applying more pressure.

I had been on the fence about buying a house in general, given a few different factors. One was that we were in California, the most expensive state in the nation for real estate. We were middle class, and I didn't see the point of bending over backwards and torturing ourselves just for the privilege of someday becoming house-poor. Life is too short for that.

But Fang's demands grew more insistent as time went on. So I reluctantly agreed to begin saving up for a down payment.

That was a fool's errand. A month later, I saw a new Movato watch sitting on her night table. That's a luxury brand. I searched online for that model and found that it retailed for about twelve hundred dollars.

Fang came home that evening. "Tell me about that new watch," I said.

"I always wanted to buy it, so I finally did," she replied casually.

"But you demanded that we save up for a down payment on a house," I said, incredulous. "I've been packing lunches for a month to save money."

"I've been waiting for this watch to go on sale for *two years*!" she screamed. "I deserve to have it!"

Right then, I nixed the house. I couldn't see myself going into an enormous mortgage with someone who had zero financial discipline. She would always be financially irresponsible. Nothing would change that.

The more I got to know my wife, the less I trusted her.

———

Baby drama wasn't much of an issue, because she never really made up her mind about that.

Early on, Fang was opposed to having children. Then she became undecided. By the last two months of our relationship—when she was losing her mind—she was erupting with baby fever.

When I reminded her that she needed to have sex with me if she wanted to make a baby, she walked out of the room without a word.

———

Maybe the most seditious of her offenses was the way that she secretly tried to get between me and my family.

I didn't know this until after the divorce, but Fang had been making phone calls to my mother behind my back and telling her secrets about our relationship. Once, during a visit back in Michigan, I'd gone to bed around one o'clock in the morning, my usual bedtime. Fang, however, had kept my mom awake until four o'clock in the morning, telling her histrionic stories about her destitute childhood.

That was horseshit. Fang's childhood wasn't destitute. Her parents were two community college teachers who'd handled their money well and now owned three investment properties. In fact, after our divorce, my mother told me that she hadn't known how to handle the bullshit this blonde hellion was flinging at her that night.

The dark truth is that Fang was trying to drive a wedge between me and my own mother. The even darker truth, I suspect, is that she was looking to get her hands on my family's estate.

Exploitation, manipulation, greed.

13

FANG: THE INEVITABLE COLLAPSE

The end, when it came, was both expected and unexpected.

Our dead bedroom was completely her fault. I say this as objectively as possible, and it doesn't matter if you don't believe me. Fang had physically shut down on me. Her hormonal profile looked like a Jackson Pollock painting. There was no amount of massages or candles or cleaned dishes or weekend getaways that would turn her libido back on.

I looked and acted the same as I always had. I did a good share of the housework. I bought flowers every Sunday, which she'd bragged about to her friends. In fact, my steadiness seemed to be the problem. Fang began complaining about my hair color, my body type, my kissing style—none of which had changed, but all of which she suddenly criticized. I asked her if there was anything about me that she found attractive anymore. She never answered.

If you've been around a woman in the process of destroying her marriage, then you know exactly what this looks and sounds like.

That said, we had one final good weekend together, on

Labor Day, playing in the sand and swimming in the waters of northern Michigan. We felt the way we'd been seven years earlier.

But that was an extinction burst. Shortly afterwards, Fang had a job interview at Magento, a B2B e-commerce platform. This was 2013, and e-commerce was in its toddler stage. She was interviewing for a sales rep position. As best I could, I helped prep her for the job interview. I quizzed her on LAMP stacks.

When she landed the job, she was ecstatic. Then she quickly started to lose her mind.

I say that cautiously, but it was true: I watched her become mentally unhinged, for lack of a better word. She was experiencing success and prestige and money and glory —all her deepest needs. They awakened in her something that had been dormant the previous seven years.

That thing was full-on narcissism.

Every day, she came home from work on a bizarre high. It was the type of high that a person with a Cluster-B personality disorder exhibits in the throes of her dysfunction. I soon found out that Magento was mostly male employees. She was one of only two or three women in the office. And Fang liked to dress beautifully, in Marc Jacobs handbags and shoes and smart outfits.

I put all the pieces together. My then-wife was obtaining narcissistic supply from the men in her office. She was vacuuming up their adoration for her own emotional needs. This meant that she could discard me, who wasn't needed for narcissistic supply any longer.

In November, I said to somebody on the phone that I wasn't sure my marriage was going to survive this. I was right.

Our final three months are a blur of dysfunction in my

memory. I found out later that she'd been going to her friend Michelle—the same one that I'd banned from my house for her abusive treatment of her boyfriend Landon— for advice about our marriage. You can guess what her advice was.

Leave him.

There's a subset of unhappy women who love nothing more than to pour gasoline on their best friends' marriages and light a match. Michelle was one of those.

Fang left for work excited every day. The seeds of inter-personal exploitation had already been present for years but they found fresh, fertile ground in her new role as a B2B salesperson. She began using phrases like *churn and burn, baby*. She wasn't happy with a set of second-place steak knives. She needed the Cadillac El Dorado.

The holidays came and went. Christmas Day was over 90 degrees Fahrenheit at her family's house in San Diego and I wore a red Santa hat with my swimsuit. I felt a weird tension in the air. I couldn't put a finger on it. Her dad handed me a glass of scotch at one pm, in the heat, and I passed out by three o'clock. I can't handle scotch and don't know why I accepted it.

January flew past, and Fang's behavior grew a bit more bizarre. At one point, I watched her clutch her head in her hands and heard her say *There's something changing inside my head and I don't know what it is*. Today she would deny it, but that would be false. In the background I could almost hear the *aroogah-aroogah* of the submarine warning siren.

A week later, I was typing on my laptop at our new dining room table. She'd found it that summer, along with a matching cabinet, and begged me to chip in half of the cost. I'd agreed.

I looked up and saw Fang staring at me from the couch. She had a weird look in her eyes.

"What?" I said.

She said simply, "I wish you'd do something wrong, so I'd have a reason to leave you."

That set me back. Try to put yourself in that situation. What do you say when your spouse tells you that she's ready to leave, all she needs is a reason? *Oh honey, I'm sorry —I'll try to be a worse partner in the future.*

I could read the tea leaves. She was putting me on notice that an exit strategy was forming. She wanted to justify her feelings but couldn't, no matter how hard she tried.

————

Two WEEKS LATER, Fang stopped hugging me. Her arms hung limply by her sides when I squeezed her. And a week after that, on the night of Saturday, February 8, she went out to a club to celebrate a milestone: She'd just received her first quarterly bonus. It was somewhere around eight thousand dollars.

Her sluttiest friend, Lisa, went with her.

Lisa was a heavyset blonde with an enormous pair of natural boobs that Fang lived in awe of and made jokes about. She'd been sharing an apartment with her music-industry boyfriend for a year, and Lisa paid him rent in daily blowjobs. She also cheated on him, which I'd discovered a year earlier when a drunken Fang allowed both a drunken Lisa and a drunken guy to come back to our apartment. The less said about that night, the better.

Fang had been living vicariously through Lisa.

I don't know what happened in that club on the night of

February 8, but Fang didn't come home that night. She didn't reply to my text messages either. I fell asleep at three in the morning, disturbed.

Fang finally did arrive home at eight o'clock am. She looked frazzled. Sunlight streaming through the windows, she sat down at our new dining room table, still in her club-wear from the night before, put her elbows on its surface, and buried her face in her hands. I sat across from her. Then she opened her hands, took a deep breath, and stated very calmly that she was leaving me.

This had been a long time coming, but I was still a bit surprised. In fact, it took a few minutes for me to process. I halfheartedly argued for a little while. I asked if she'd thought this all the way through. I meekly noted that we hadn't finished watching a television series together, which stands as the stupidest thing I've ever uttered. But in very short order—in less than fifteen minutes, for sure—I'd sunk back on our cold gray love seat and laced my hands behind my head and accepted it.

I couldn't find any reasons to protest. I didn't want her in my life anymore. She'd become a liability in every way.

The next night, she tried to start a fight with me. I sat on the same cold gray love seat while she stood over me asking, *Why don't you divorce me?* She repeated the demand again and again: *Why don't you divorce me? Why don't you divorce me?*

I refused to take the bait; fighting was pointless. I also didn't understand the timing. Something in her brain was broken. Just one day before, she'd announced that she was leaving me. Now she was demanding that I divorce her, flipping around the roles in the situation. My best guess is that she was trying to project the responsibility for destroying the marriage onto me. She dreaded the idea of being perceived as less than perfect. This way, she could preserve her fragile sense of self and continue to feel superior to everyone in the world. Or maybe she was just practical, hoping I would pay for the divorce process.

We coexisted for the next three weeks while she looked for a new place to live. I slept on the couch, as men are taught to do, only getting up after she'd left for work at seven-thirty. At the manager's office, I took her name off the lease and drafted a new one with me as the sole occupant of the apartment. (A year and a half later, that turned out to be a lucrative move worth nearly four thousand dollars.)

One night during that time, she looked over her accounts, and announced out loud that we were even, financially.

I wanted to strangle her.

Over the last few years, I'd contributed about $2100 per month to the shared bills—rent and farmer's market purchases—plus another $300 per month to pay off her credit card debt. That made a monthly total of $2400, give or take. At the same time, her total monthly contribution to the household, as far as I knew, was about $800, in utilities and grocery purchases. Let's assume I was wrong and that she paid more. Even if she'd been paying $1200 per month, this was still a very lopsided arrangement. I was paying at least twice as much as she was. This ratio had worked at the start of the relationship, when she made about half of my income. However, in the last couple of years, our income had evened out. We were both making the same amount of money since she'd started working at the shipping company. But she'd shrewdly refused to renegotiate this arrangement.

She was that kind of bitch. The moment she declared us "financially even", it took every ounce of my self-control to walk out of the room. Fang lived inside a distorted-reality field that wouldn't allow reason to penetrate it. She had been exploiting me, and I'd been letting it happen, assuming she would reciprocate someday.

That wouldn't happen.

I didn't want to fight. I didn't need to show her that I was morally right and that she was morally wrong. I just wanted her out of my life.

On the weekend of March 1, she finally moved out. I think her family helped her in the move, but I'll never know. I spent the weekend sitting in a hotel room at the BLVD Hotel on Ventura near Universal City.

That Sunday night, I arrived home at six o'clock pm. I walked into my apartment and found the place half empty.

We hadn't communicated about what she was planning to take with her, so it was a surprise to see the new dining room set gone and the entire master bedroom empty. All she'd left me was the living room furniture, television, bookshelves, spare bed, and one cat. I went into the kitchen and found that she'd taken everything there too. In the now-empty cupboard lay a few cheap plates, cheap plastic glasses, and cheap utensils. They looked new; her mother had probably bought those things for me. I like to interpret it as a final apology for her daughter's behavior.

Walking through the empty unit, I heard the heels of my dress shoes echo loudly on the hardwood floor. I felt a sense of relief. The weight had been lifted off my shoulders. The egotistical greedy tiger who'd tried to slice me to ribbons had finally been let out of my house, the door closed.

I wasn't sad at all. In fact, I felt ecstatic. This came as a surprise, because I hadn't admitted to myself just how unhappy I'd become.

———

FANG MOVED into an apartment a few blocks away. Over the next three months, I occasionally drove past her on the street. At night, she peppered me with pathetic text messages like *Are you going to hate me for the rest of your life?*

I never replied. She was clearly wracked with guilt. That was good. She needed to be.

One time, she called me, and I decided to pick up. It turned out that she wanted to know my plans.

"I'm staying in California until May fifteenth," I said, "then I'm leaving."

"For how long?"

"Permanently."

"And where are you going?" she asked.

"That's none of your business. You can reach me by email."

"Well, I was wondering if you'd like to split the cost of the divorce."

"No," I answered.

"Why not?"

"Because this was all your idea. You started destroying this marriage from the first week it was born. Now you'll carry it all the way to the end. It's totally on you. And if you don't divorce me, then we will stay legally married forever. Is that what you want?"

She didn't reply. I'd successfully called her bluff.

"Do you have any more questions?" I said. "You have five seconds."

I counted down *five, four, three, two, one,* while she sputtered. Then I ended the call without a word. Message delivered.

It wasn't the last time we spoke, though. I ran into her one final time, at the Studio City Farmers' Market. This was a few weeks before I left the city. I had decided to move back to the Midwest after thirteen long years on the West Coast.

When I saw her, I was taken aback. Fang looked like a skeleton. She had easily lost twenty pounds, and she now looked almost frail. I like to think it was the stress of divorcing a good man for no justifiable reason. But this weight loss could have been caused by more severe mental-health issues. I'll never know.

I walked up to her and said, "I have nothing to say to you."

She replied, "I'm not asking you to."

I moved along without looking back. I should've told her that I'd see her next Tuesday. But these are things we think of later.

That was the last time in my life that I saw or spoke with my ex-wife. There were a couple of exchanged emails that summer, and a package containing the final divorce decree arrived in December.

Nine months after she walked out, I was free. The divorce only cost me a few dollars in photocopies and postage, but the marriage had cost me a lot more than that. It would take me two years, one sabbatical, thousands of miles traveled, and many experiences with other women before my anger subsided and I felt like myself again.

But even then, I knew that she'd changed me.

14

FANG: THE FALLOUT AND THE FAREWELL

The following year, I moved to Chicago to start my life over. There, I started dating a couples' therapist. Her name was Sarah. She was 44 years old, five years older than me at the time.

I didn't date Sarah because she was a therapist. But her career turned out to be the defining aspect of our relationship.

For several months, she occasionally popped over to my new home, a renovated 2-bedroom, 3-bath condo in Uptown. It was located five miles north of the Loop. In the 1920s, this neighborhood had been the art deco and entertainment center of the city. If you're familiar with Chicago, I lived just three blocks from the historic Green Mill jazz club and the Aragon Theater. Sarah lived one mile west of me, in Ravenswood, but she was protective of her privacy and never invited me to her home.

Over dinners, we talked a lot about psychology and human relationships. Sarah introduced me to the work of John Gottman, the famous couples' therapist who popularized the so-called Four Horsemen of the Apocalypse: criticism, contempt, defensiveness, and stonewalling. The presence of any of those predicted divorce, especially contempt.

I hadn't known about the four major attachment styles either—secure, anxious, avoidant, and disorganized—but Sarah opened my eyes to those too. She talked about her boots-on-the-ground clinical experience with Cluster-B types, noting that borderline personality disorder was the most difficult to treat. And she talked frequently about the challenges presented to couples in the black community. Sarah was white, but navigating stresses unique to black couples occupied a large part of her practice.

We talked a lot about Fang. I told Sarah that we didn't have to talk about my ex-wife, that I didn't expect it, that she was off the clock. But she liked to help people with their relationship problems, including the men she was sleeping with. So I talked and talked. She noted that Fang was emotionally dysregulated but didn't elaborate further. She asked questions about my childhood, which I slowly realized was not exactly as perfect as I'd always assumed. After all, the people-pleasing that I'd sometimes indulged in came from somewhere, as did my decision to marry someone as difficult as Fang.

With Sarah's help, it slowly dawned on me that I had spent the last twenty years of my adult life leaving myself open to dangerous or bad women, some of whom had hurt me.

I needed to close that gate. So I did.

Emotionally, I sealed myself off. I stopped giving so much of myself to other people, especially to undeserving women. Instead, I learned to guard my energy, and deliver it only to those people who deserve it.

If you're a heterosexual woman struggling to find love in

the dating market, I probably come off like the type of guy you want to avoid. You might argue that most adult American men already wall themselves off from other people. You could point out the vast number of adult men who are out of touch with their emotions. You could say that aging men should learn to open themselves up to new people and new ideas, to avoid stagnation.

Overall, you'd probably be right about those things. Look at a film like *Garden State*: a manic pixie dream girl (played by Natalie Portman) teaches a closed-off and depressed male protagonist (played by Zach Braff) how to open up.

But I'm built different. Unlike other men, I was plenty open. Instead, I needed to learn to protect myself.

Sarah and I lasted about six months. Eventually she went her way, and I went mine. But I will always be thankful for her insights.

————

IT SEEMS that almost everybody who's ever broken up with another person says that their ex was a narcissist. Some are exaggerating to gain pity, to play the victim. A few are just straight up lying, to cover their own mistakes or duplicity.

I'm not doing those things. Fang was truly a narcissist.

At Sarah the therapist's suggestion, I went to the DSM-V, which is the national manual for classifying and diagnosing mental disorders. Under narcissism, there is a checklist of nine different possible traits. To be diagnosed, you need to exhibit five of the nine criteria.

With the therapist at my side, I went down the list with a finger, thinking about my ex-wife:

- A grandiose sense of self-importance
- A preoccupation with fantasies of unlimited success, power, brilliance, beauty, or ideal love
- A belief that he or she is special and unique and can only be understood by, or should associate with, other special or high-status people or institutions
- A need for excessive admiration
- A sense of entitlement
- Interpersonally exploitive behavior
- A lack of empathy
- Envy of others or a belief that others are envious of him or her
- A demonstration of arrogant and haughty behaviors or attitudes

According to my tabulation, she scored a 9 out of 9. This meant that Fang was a perfect narcissist, at least by the end of the relationship.

This is not an exaggeration. All nine traits had been present in her personality, at one time or another, to greater or lesser degrees. Even if I give her the benefit of the doubt and deleted two of the least present traits, she still scored 7 of 9. That is still more than enough to qualify.

Yes, I had married a narcissist.

But I hadn't known that initially. Early on, I'd thought her behavior was just immaturity. As time went on, those traits didn't go away. Fang never matured. Instead, her dysfunctional behavior grew worse.

Many of us hear *omg my ex was such a narcissist* from single or divorced friends. If this makes you roll your eyes, let me offer a simple explanation: you hear this a lot *because narcissists really do destroy a lot of relationships.*

They wear down their spouses or partners with egotism, manipulation, and greed. Once you've boarded that train, splitsville is the final destination. So if people say their ex-partner was a narcissist, give them the benefit of the doubt. It's often true.

I used to think that Fang's prior promiscuity was the cause of our divorce. When I met her, she already had a high body count. I never knew the exact number, but she once confessed that she banged fifteen guys just in the one year before meeting me. She would deny that today, but she said it to my face—and when a man hears that, he doesn't forget it.

But gradually I realized that I was wrong. Fang's promiscuity wasn't the cause of our divorce, and it didn't ruin her personality as so many red-pill guys would like to have you believe. That's backwards. Fang's sexual aggressiveness was the *result* of her impulsive and uncontrollable personality, which had existed from birth. Like her father, Fang was driven towards wild risks, including getting tattoos, using cocaine, and reckless driving. These behaviors grew out of the traits baked into her DNA, not anything else.

———

IN THE END, I escaped a horrific time in my life with relatively little damage.

Why? Because I'm a tough dude, mentally and emotionally. I don't let monstrous or abusive people push me around; I thank my mother for this backbone. Less sturdy men are eaten alive by women like my ex-wife. It happens to millions of us across the world every day.

Because of Fang, I learned pretty much every lesson a

man can learn about women and relationships. Some of them I'd already known. Some I hadn't.

I've been very fortunate in life so far, but that marriage stands as the worst thing that's ever happened to me. I welcomed a tiger into my house, and I paid the price when it ripped up my furniture and pissed all over the floor. In a weird way, however, she was the best thing to ever happen to me. The end of the relationship put everything into stark relief. It made me discover my own needs, priorities, and limits.

Afterwards, I didn't grow bitter towards women either. I wouldn't let that happen. But I did carry anger towards her, as an individual, for a long time. For a full year after the divorce, I would pace around my new home in Chicago, alone, lecturing my ex-wife out loud, talking to the air.

You don't want that kind of anger. It's not fun.

I eventually got through it by layering slabs of new experience onto myself, like building a lasagna. I went to South America for four months. I lifted weights four days a week and added 25 pounds of muscle onto my body. I found new girlfriends. I found a new job as a ghostwriter and wrote forty new books. I became fluent in Spanish. I made many new international friends. I began playing full-field soccer again. I started long-distance swimming. I revisited Michigan more and saw my family more often. You can read about some of these experiences in *Bold*, the companion memoir to this one.

Eventually, recurring images of Fang disappeared from my head. Her face has mostly receded into the mists of time. I learned that you don't need to forgive a person if you just forget about her. The effect is the same either way.

———

FANG REMARRIED eight months after our divorce was finalized.

Her second husband is a Mexican immigrant named Santiago, who had once played water polo for the Mexican national team. Fang's dad, a water polo coach, had been Santiago's coach at his community college. In fact, I remembered her dad mentioning the older Mexican player whose example was elevating the younger players on the team. I'd never met the guy, though I did know his brother a little. Fang used to visit San Diego without me every month or two, so it's possible she met him during our marriage.

This begs the million-dollar question: Did Fang have an affair with this guy prior to the end of our marriage? I don't know. She claimed that there was no one else, and I have no reason to disbelieve her. But people often lie as a part of their mating strategies, especially when they're unhappy with their spouses.

It doesn't matter now.

Fang and Santiago had a child. I feel sorry for that little girl, because being raised by a narcissistic mother is a rough way to start your life. Look online for the human wreckage created by such parents. You can find them on Reddit, YouTube, and elsewhere, posting comments about going no-contact and re-raising themselves minus the dysfunction.

My message to Santiago: You chose poorly, buddy. As did I, but you were dumber than me, because you got her pregnant.

I can only imagine how tortured his life is at this point. He's a community college water polo coach—same as his father-in-law—trapped in what appears to be a green-card marriage to a high-earning but toxic and middle-aged blonde corporate saleswoman who hates men. She has almost certainly dangled her control of his immigration status over his head.

I hope that I'm wrong. I hope they have a deeply fulfilling relationship based on mutual trust and respect.

But I know her.

————

AFTER IT ENDED, I didn't immediately reject the idea of a second marriage, like so many divorced men do. I function well in a stable, monogamous relationship. For happiness and productivity, it's the best.

However, I now had better screening abilities. I decided that I would only remarry if I could find a specific type of woman. So I made a list of four non-negotiable qualities.

- **My second wife would come from a foreign country**. Because of Fang, I'd become deathly allergic to entitled American women. They made my skin crawl.
- **My second wife would come from a somewhat conservative family**. I don't mean conservative in voting record, but in behavior. I wanted a normal group of in-laws. I didn't want couches burning in driveways and motorcross bikes plunging down mine shafts.
- **My second wife would have to be unconcerned with social media**. Good luck with that, right?
- **My second wife would have to be younger than me**. I was turning 40 years old. While I didn't have a specific age in mind, I

knew that younger was mandatory if there was
going to be a hope for children.

I told people this list of qualities, knowing that finding a
woman with all of these qualities would be next to impossible. And if I did find a woman like that, she probably
wouldn't be interested in me.

So I shelved the thought of remarriage. It just wasn't
going to be in the cards.

Like so many other things, I was wrong about that too.

Six years after my divorce, in 2020, I found a woman
with all four of these qualities. To my surprise, she loved me
as much as I loved her. We traveled the world together for
two years, an epic start to our epic romance.

Eight years after my divorce, in 2023, I married this
outstanding young lady, and committed myself to her. My
second marriage has been the polar opposite of my first.
Ashley is everything I ever wanted—sweet, respectful, kind,
highly intelligent, sexy, funny, talented, and creative. She's
been the greatest blessing of my adult life.

15

THREE DEAD FRIENDSHIPS, THREE CAUSES OF DEATH

I can see Kevin prancing around the backyard, delivering long, intense lectures to himself. Even at age six, he was famous for his mental obsessions, ranging from Greek mythology to Disney World. We were born two months apart, but I was a year ahead of him in school.

For the next five years, Kevin and I spent two hours a day together at the home of a Lebanese woman, Mrs. Baroody. She took care of a group of children after school, a home child care, though I soon came to regard her as my second mother. In fact, she and my real mother ended up becoming best friends, until Mrs. Baroody's death from lung cancer at just over fifty years old. She smoked two packs a day.

If a person can be described in a single adjective, Kevin was *smart*. He was slave to his maddening brain. He wasn't athletic, but he spent five years challenging me in mental games. I loved having him around. Our big thing after school was watching Inspector Gadget and having ridiculous debates about esoteric topics like killer bees.

In warmer weather we played outside a lot. Kevin and I spent part of our summers romping through the field behind the Baroody house. We found a nudie magazine out there, titled *Foxes*, the first either of us had seen. "Um, I don't think we should be looking at this," he said, worried.

Soon we decided to build a fort in a copse of trees. We bought cheap statues of cats for a dollar each at a local garage sale in the subdivision, then rolled them down the street back to the Baroody house, where we dragged them into the field and set up them up as the guardians of our little summer citadel. Through it all, Kevin kept up a steady stream of commentary. I ran my mouth too, but his ran faster.

By middle school, the after-school care was unnecessary, and we left the Baroody house and went our separate ways. His father died of a sudden heart attack when we were fourteen, but I didn't go to the funeral, for reasons I can't remember. We reconnected after college: he'd graduated from University of Michigan School of Law in record time and went to work as an attorney in suburban Detroit.

Throughout our twenties and thirties, our relationship grew one-sided. I never heard from him unless I initiated communication first. A response wasn't guaranteed either. Often my text messages or phone calls went unanswered. If I was lucky, a month or two later he would apologize.

He did reach out occasionally. One year, he invited me to play in a Thanksgiving football game, which was a nice gesture. We went out one night in Los Angeles, during his work trip. And I agreed to host a weird friend of his on my sofa who had decided to move to Los Angeles, though the friend went AWOL and wouldn't answer his phone or reply to my messages.

Anyways, after twenty years of dragging the relationship along, I finally had enough.

During my divorce, at age 39, I'd started cutting ties
with people who hadn't been there for me, or people to
whom I'd been too loyal to for too long. I didn't cut out
Kevin, not right away, but I decided to quietly test him. I
saw him at a wedding, and as usual he apologized for being
terrible at keeping up with me. He promised to do better.

"All right," I said.

Later that week, I deleted his number from my phone.

It wasn't because I didn't like him. I've always loved
chatting with Kevin. We have a great chemistry. He can
quote *The Room* a bit too often for my taste, but he defi-
nitely has no shortage of thoughts.

No, I deleted his number just to see if he would keep his
promise.

He never did.

That was a decade ago. He never bothered to communicate with me again. When I dropped the reins, the relationship instantly died.

This really pisses me off, for one simple reason: we don't
get do-overs on childhood friends. I can't go back to age six
and make new first-grade friends again. I hear that a
common regret of elderly people in the U.S. is that they
didn't stay in touch with friends and loved ones. He'll defi-
nitely be one of those people.

It's not clear why Kevin let me go. One is that he is
mentally self-absorbed. This is the most likely explanation.
Another is that he's unhappy with his own wife-and-two-
kids suburban existence that he created for himself, and I
stand as an example of how different life can be. A third is
that his difficult, nagging mother pecked all the will-to-
communicate out of him. A fourth is that he had some kind

of breakdown as he approached the same age at which his father suddenly died.

We have mutuals, so there is a good chance I run into Kevin again in the future. I won't confront him about any of this. I'll just nod, smile, and keep my life private from him.

Someone once said that there are two types of people: those who give their energy, and those who guard their energy. I've given this guy more than enough of my energy in my life. I wish he'd given me more of his.

———

SHE WAS NEARLY six feet tall, with a big mane of blonde hair, and strong tan legs that seemed to go on forever up to her black suede miniskirt.

I couldn't keep my eyes off her.

It was orientation day at my university, and I was sitting with a hundred other students and all of our parents in a lecture hall. We were listening to the head of the honors program welcome us and describe what we could expect from our coursework. Fifteen of the students in the room were recipients of full-tuition scholarships handed out by Catholic archdioceses all over the country. I wondered if she were one of them.

"How many of you, by show of hands, are taking all three courses that the honors program offers?" the head said. "Triple-trackers, hands up, please!"

I raised my hand. I looked over. Blondie was raising her hand too. That meant that she was smart.

My dad's elbow landed in my ribs. "Hey," he whispered, "did you see that girl? She's gonna be in all your classes. Lucky dog!"

I shrunk down in my seat. My old man had scoped out Blondie too. We were cut from the same cloth.

For the next hour, visions of what could be danced through my head. I was seventeen years old, so you can probably imagine what those were.

Later that day, I introduced myself to her. From the moment she opened her mouth, those boy's dreams flew straight out the window, never to be seen again.

Blondie was a very different type of person.

———

You EVER MEET an attractive person who you have zero romantic chemistry with? That was Sabina.

She was a southern belle, hailing from the southern portion of the southern state of South Carolina.

Sabina had impeccable manners, a slow and deliberate way of speaking, and a habit of looking at you as if you were a specimen and she were studying you from a great distance. Cerebral and odd, Sabina loved to think. It was her favorite activity. She'd sit back, cross her legs, cast her eyes up to the ceiling of the room, and begin to toy with an invisible thought. She'd spin it around, study it from seven different angles. She'd sometimes even pause a conversation in order to think a bit more. Have you ever met anybody who asks you to wait while she thinks about something? It's bizarre.

I didn't mind, though. She was utterly unlike anyone I'd ever known. She carried her own salad dressing everywhere she went because, in her words, "you never know". She refused to eat food at the dining hall and escaped the campus the moment she was able to. She referred to the Civil War as "the War of Northern Aggression". She was a proclaimed Anglophile who claimed that there had to be objective basis for the superiority of the British Empire. For a class project, she even interviewed the ninety-something Senator Strom Thurmond (R - SC), the most segregationist politician in the twentieth-century history of Congress. He petted her hair and told her she was beautiful.

Most of all, Sabina was caught between word and image. On one hand, she was an English major, like me, but she also double-majored in art history. Both ways of seeing the world seized her brain. She immersed herself in medieval illuminated manuscripts, but she also never encountered an obscure European novelist who she wouldn't give a try.

I spent many hours studying with Sabina in her dorm room, either sitting on her bed or on her floor. The first couple of years, we shared four of our five classes each semester, so our academic overlap was enormous. We had complementary talents. She was better at philosophy and visual analysis than I was, but I was better at story structure, grammar, and historical analysis. I was a moderate liberal, and she was a proud conservative. Given her state of origin, that is no surprise at all.

We were both competitors and collaborators. She and I even went to Oxford University together during our junior year. I remember thinking that she might never come home, because that place ticked all her boxes so thoroughly, but she did return. (You can read more about my experiences there in *The Oxford Diaries*.)

Later, in our senior year, Sabina moved into an off-campus apartment, alone, which she turned into a painting studio. There, she began to lose her mind. She created some great canvases at that time, a couple of which still stick with me today. But she claimed to see shadows following her at the edges of the living room. I was skeptical until I went over there one night and was instantly hit with a feeling of violence and dread. Something supernatural was in that apartment, for sure. Sabina was relieved that I felt it too. Later, she found out that a person had been murdered in the unit a few months before she moved in.

Sabina never openly dated anybody on campus during the four years we spent together, but I suspect she had some clandestine hookups that she didn't breathe a word about. Discretion was the name of her game.

But she did have some surprises up her sleeve. In March of our freshman year, I asked her what she was doing for spring break.

"I'm going to Brazil," she replied.

I hadn't been expecting that. "For what?"

"The guy I've been seeing moved there and invited me to join him."

"You've been seeing a guy?"

"Yes."

"Who is he?"

She paused and looked a bit guilty. I hadn't seen her like this. "My high school history teacher."

I forced her to tell me more. It turned out that this teacher, age twenty-nine, had left the school at the same time that she had graduated, a year earlier. He'd stayed in touch with her over the summer—she'd already turned eighteen in May—and the two had started clandestinely dating during our first semester of college. Then he'd moved to Brazil in January and told her to come visit him on spring break. He'd sent her a round-trip airplane ticket.

I told her to have fun. I didn't really know what to feel. This was way outside of my own experience at the time.

Two weeks later, Sabina came back from Brazil. She

announced that it'd been a disaster, because she found out that he'd been dating other girls in Rio de Janeiro. That seemed like an obvious assumption to me, even at my young age.

"I was so stupid," she said.

"Well, you got to see Brazil," I said.

Her head was in the clouds, but she wasn't immune to pleasures of the flesh. We spent a week in Rome together, where she got so drunk on red wine that I had to carry her back to her rented room. Totally plastered, she tried to take off her shirt and grab me, but I disengaged. It's very bad form—and illegal—to take advantage of drunk girls, especially one who trusts you. I put her to bed, gave her a bottle of water, and placed a trash can on the floor next to her. Outside her door, I waited in the hallway, listening. As soon as I heard the vomiting begin, I left.

People often thought we were a couple. We did look like a match. We were both tall and athletic, both light-haired, both textual, both artistic. And we spent a lot of time together. Sabina's mother seemed to take a special interest in me, and I liked chatting with her salt-of-the-earth father. But she and I were never a couple, not even for one night, and we never would be.

After graduation, Sabina headed back home to teach at a local college in South Carolina. I took the Amtrak down south to visit her once. I stayed with her in her small house in Charleston, alone, chatting about the future over candle-light. She said that her brother predicted that I would win a Pulitzer Prize. That was very nice, but I took it with a grain of salt, considering I'd never even met the guy. Later, after she'd moved to New York to attend art school, I spent a couple nights staying with her in Brooklyn Heights, age twenty-four.

That was the last time I saw her. I moved to California and tried to keep in touch, but she began to grow even more eccentric than before. Her painting career took off, and she won a Fulbright scholarship that took her to China for a while. Later, she was hired as a lecturer at a pair of prestigious universities in Boston.

The last time she emailed me, she said that she was temporarily moving to London for some kind of opportunity. But she was vague about what it was, when it would end, and when she would return.

I decided to let her go. I was 31 years old, engaged to another woman, living on the opposite end of the country from her. Plus, I could tell when a person was trying to squirm out of a relationship. If she wanted a friendship, she could have it, but I wouldn't ask or initiate.

Sabina never communicated with me again.

It was strange. We shared so many interests and so much educational history that Sabina's disappearance from my life confused me. I found out later that there was a man in London that she was interested in, and they subsequently married.

Hence the vagueness about her intentions there.

It's possible that, in her mind, Sabina had been keeping me on a back burner as a possible life partner. *Break glass for spare husband.* If so, maybe she lost interest in me when I got engaged. Or when she found a guy that better suited her. On the other hand, it's possible that her husband didn't want her communicating with me, or other men. I'll never know. People like her are better left to float away on their own unusual trajectories.

Today, Sabina lives outside of Boston, where she is an accomplished studio artist and a humanities lecturer at two very recognized universities. Mutuals tell me that she's happy.

———

I CALLED him the Victorian Gent.

His name was Nick, another college classmate. A beefy guy from upstate New York, he had a Venezuelan mother and white father, whom he never talked about. My friends were his friends, so we became friends by default. You know that type of relationship. It probably wouldn't have happened any other way.

Nick was a diligent student. His dream was to become a doctor, but he worried that he didn't have the grades for it. As a result, he spent so much time studying on the second floor of the university library that people began seeking him out there.

He carried himself with a weird formality. He claimed to be a conservative and loudly announced all the usual right-wing beliefs about women, families, and sexuality. At the same time, he loved the buffoonish David Lee Roth of Van Halen, claiming that he was the best rock frontman ever. (I was team Sammy.) Nick would mouth platitudes about moral correctness and the importance of good living, then get wasted on one-dollar happy hour drink specials at off-campus college bars.

The Victorian Gent objected to some of my more liberal or progressive views about human society. For my part, I noticed his obnoxious little spiteful cackle of a laugh that seemed to reveal a truer spirit lurking deep inside of him.

People in espionage stress the importance of listening to your intuition. If something feels off, that's because something is being concealed. Here's what I'm trying to say:

Something didn't hang right about him. I felt that Nick wasn't behaving authentically. His words and manner didn't seem to match his true self.

Nonetheless, Nick and I grew close. He was a good guitarist, like me, and we taught each other some stuff. He showed me how to play "Hot For Teacher", a non-conservative song if there ever was one. I helped him brainstorm and structure his medical school application essays when he had trouble figuring out what to say. In fact, I overslept the morning I had volunteered to drive him to his MCAT exam. I apologized for that later with endless pitchers of beer. I don't like to let people down.

Graduation came and went, and Nick and I saw each other a few times in our twenties, like so many college friends do. We stayed in occasional touch until our mid-thirties, when he got married. I was invited to the wedding, so I flew across the country, to Florida, where he'd established himself as a chiropractor just north of Miami. He'd never been able to get into medical school and flunked out of osteopath school as well.

At the wedding, I was surprised to see his father—the one he'd never talked about—in a wheelchair, barely able to speak. He'd been suffering a decades-long chronic illness. Suddenly, a few things about Nick started to make sense. I introduced myself to his new blonde wife who spoke with a Venezuelan accent, congratulated them, and made my way back to the hotel that night.

What remained of our friendship was ended by politics.

Most Americans have lost at least one friend or family member to MAGA delusions. It seized the nation like a fever dream. In 2016, Nick and I started messaging again, and he started making jabs at "Obummer" and complaining about Nancy Pelosi. He claimed to hate the Affordable

Care Act, even though he was a medical professional. He'd shown zero interest in this type of politics before, so something had shifted inside him.

I finally called him, frustrated, and we had a bare-knuckled verbal political fight on the phone. His tone was hostile and angry and vicious, a million miles away from the stuffy Victorian Gent he'd pretended to be while in college. He mocked and belittled me and my views. I asked him what type of media he'd been consuming, which he refused to answer. Then he said some mildly racist stuff, which I've blocked from my memory. When I told him it was mildly racist, he replied that he couldn't be racist because he employed an Iranian immigrant at his office.

The icing on this poisonous cake was the moment that he derided me as just a college friend, as though a *college friend* is somebody less than human. I quickly reminded Nick that this college friend had paid over a thousand dollars to attend his wedding, and that he had not done the same for mine.

He didn't have a response to that. We hung up, angry.

A mutual told me that Nick had called him a few days later, still angry, demanding explanations about some of the stuff we'd said.

"He sounded really hostile," my friend said, who stopped speaking to him at that point.

The death of my friendship with Nick is a tiny microcosm of what's happened to the United States since 2016. People with pre-existing hostility or oppositional personalities have seized upon politics to exaggerate and focus all their grievances. It's no different from the radicalization that happens to people of religious faiths in other parts of the world. In fact, the exact nature of the lens doesn't even matter. It could be cooking, music, books, or television shows. People struggling with inner rage use any vehicle they can find to vent their anger.

Nick has three children now, which I hope means that he no longer has time to read Daily Caller or watch Newsmax.

I won't make a Florida Man joke. But please notice that none of this spite erupted out of him until he moved to that state. Draw your own conclusions.

16

FINAL WORDS

My wife is from Barbados, a distant island in the southeastern part of the Caribbean.

Add up all my time there, and I've spent a total of about two years of my life on that beautiful hunk of rock. But being there drives me a little batty sometimes. Island fever is real: I get restless. More than once I've lifted off that runway at Grantley International Airport with a big smile on my face and a vision of jackets, bonfires, and winter's first snowfall dancing in my head.

But there is something remarkable about human relationships on that island. They don't disappear. People don't turn their backs on one another, not in the same way as we do in the United States and elsewhere. Many Bajans still stick with the same social groups they had as children. The island is only 166 square miles, so the people know they have to cooperate with one another for that reason. In fact, they never bother to say *hey, we should get together sometime*. They know they will get together again. It's unavoidable.

Almost 300,000 people live in Barbados, ninety percent of whom are black. The other ten percent are white, Asian, Indian, and Guyanese. Inside that ten-percent community, relationships are woven together very closely. Everybody seems to be in a second-degree relationship with everybody else. Maybe you don't know the person next to you at the open-air Brighton Market on a Saturday morning, but it's guaranteed you both know someone in common.

In fact, people in the Caribbean are famous for referring to everybody as "my cousin" or "my aunty", even if they're not related. There, in the old days, when families had seven children and lived side by side in the same pocket of the island for decades, they saw no point in differentiating between blood and non-blood. It's still holds true today. Add marriages and divorces, and you've got an interesting porridge of people.

If you're a modern person whose most important rela-tionship is with your Netflix account, you likely have never known anything like this.

————

JOSEPH HEINRICH, an anthropologist at Harvard University, coined the term WEIRD to describe a partic-ular category of modern people. It stands for *Western, Educated, Industrialized, Rich,* and *Democratic.* I'm one of them, and if you're reading or listening to this, you probably are too.

We WEIRD people are excellent at economic produc-tion. We offer high-priced services to one another, and to anybody outside the WEIRD bubble who can somehow afford us. We often put our companies first, before the welfare of our people, because pushing productivity forward is the unstated main purpose of our lives. It's expected that WEIRD people work incessantly to serve the golden calf of economic success. To accomplish this, we are detail-oriented, thorough, and conscientious.

In the past, anyone who stepped outside of this Protestant work ethic bubble was shamed. That's changed somewhat, but there is still a zero percent chance that you don't know someone who's moved to a different city for a job. We accept this as a basic truth. Families split up and move thousands of miles apart. I've personally lived in five major U.S. cities.

It's partly because of our geography. The United States has benefitted from its huge, flat interior with wide, smooth rivers. In fact, the longest navigable river in the world is the Mississippi, at 2100 miles. This accident of terrain opened the economic potential of the entire interior of the country. We could produce raw ingredients, process them, add value, and ship the finished goods out of the continent. Our land is fertile, so it was easy to do this. This trade helped us innovate and gradually build our robust economy over centuries.

With such opportunities, Americans took advantage of them. One by one, we peeled off the East Coast and plunged westward, headed for a patch of free land, or a distant cattle drive, or a creek that rumor said might yield gold nuggets. In our search for opportunity, we Americans left our loved ones behind, again and again and again.

Disappearing became a part of our national character. If things don't work out, we peace out. The word today is *ghosting*. A hundred years ago, it was called *giving 'em the slip*.

I'll bet fifty bucks you've heard a conversation that goes like this—

Hey, what happened to that guy Greg who used to hang out here?

I don't know.

Really? I thought you guys were close.

No, I haven't heard from him in a couple years.

Does anybody know where he went?

Nah, he just disappeared.

Discussions like these happen all the time if you're a WEIRD, and especially if you're a white male. But they didn't used to happen this much.

We Americans used to keep tabs on one another more closely. We used to form all kind of social associations in our cities, according to one famous eagle-eyed French observer of nineteenth-century American culture.

But that has changed.

The ironic part? We've pulled apart from one another at precisely the time when we've been handed a hundred free online communication tools.

———

MY OWN VIEW is a bit more cynical: Most modern people in the developed world view friendships as *transactional*. In other words, relationships form because one person wants to quietly use the other for personal gain. This reason goes unspoken, swimming silently beneath the surface of the interactions.

Here's what's changed. Since 1945, the postwar United States has created more wealth for more people than any other society in the history of the world. We have machines to do almost every basic household task. We can find any product we want, or have it delivered to our houses, in just a few hours.

With this type of wealth and convenience, there's no need for other people, which means there is no need for friendships, not even for exploitative ones. And there's no need for lifelong marriages either. Everything and everyone can be discarded, including family—doubly so if they spout ludicrous opinions about vaccines or support felonious political candidates.

But this trend may not last forever. As the United States becomes a more unequal country—it's been trending this way for a long time—we may see interdependence quietly creeping back into the chat. The majority of us who aren't generationally wealthy could start to rediscover the value of relationships just because we *need* them. Look at truly poor countries, such as Haiti, where working towards wealth isn't an option. For those people, much of their time is occupied by relationships, for better or for worse.

Here's another thought. Maybe the sweet spot for human relationships, as a society, is during the industrialization phase of the DTM (demographic transition model). In that period, the traditional relationships of the agricultural society remain intact, even as the standard of living begins to rise. The United States experienced this from the late nineteenth century to the mid-twentieth century, the same period when we formed our many social associations.

But those days are gone. Today, we are wandering through a weird post-industrial, post-relationship, screen-mediated version of life that nobody on earth has ever experienced before.

———

LET'S CONSIDER ANOTHER CULPRIT: introversion and extroversion.

Introverts get their energy from being alone, while extroverts get their energy from being with other people. This has nothing to do with how much a person talks. In fact, there are many quiet extroverts and many talkative introverts.

The classic view of this energy spectrum is that extroverts show more positive affect, e.g. happiness, but have shorter or shallower relationships. Meanwhile, introverts often present less immediate happiness, but they often have special gifts that lead to longer relationships and a more rewarding search for meaning.

That seems mostly true, in my experience. Latin American populations are routinely rated as very happy, and countries such as the Dominican Republic and Venezuela and Argentina tend to be more extroverted than other populations. But heavily indigenous people in mountain countries such as Bolivia and Peru tend strongly towards the introverted. This illustrates the long shadow of colonialism: it can be argued that the greedy, marauding Spaniards literally brought extroversion to the quiet indigenous mountain people. (Another imperialistic indignity!) Even today, those native communities feel very quiet, even depressed. I've gone deep into the Aymara territory, exploring indigenous villages high in the Andes. Those people present exactly zero signs of happiness.

You've read the stories of my failed relationships in this book. As a borderline introvert myself, I may also have been fighting a battle against an extroverted American culture that prizes shallow relationships. It's possible that I was going to the hardware store hoping to find milk, over and over. This felt especially true in southern California, where people really do seem to view each other as disposable. It's a place where if someone says *I'll call you*, you then know with certainty that that person will never, ever speak to you again.

———

THE FINAL ASPECT TO consider in this is the effect of a narcissistic culture. Mental health experts have been sounding the alarm on this for years now. Confidence is security that is carried on the inside, but egotism and its vicious cousin narcissism are insecurity that is carried on the outside. As social media has grown, more Americans are deriving their self-image from external sources, which boosts the rate of narcissism ever higher.

But there's also evidence that the United States is growing less narcissistic. The Baby Boomers (birth years 1946 to 1964) started life with record high rates of narcissism overall, especially in displays of hypersensitivity. They've begun to die off, and a 2019 study revealed that narcissism decreases in individuals after age forty.

Either way, narcissists are everywhere, and as a victim of mild narcissistic abuse, I can vouch for the fact that the love-bombing phase is seductive and that the bad behavior only creeps in afterwards. The gaslighting, the blame shifting, the exploitation, the constant criticism, the boundary violations, the emotional rollercoaster—all these shenanigans made Fang into someone I couldn't recognize. I do feel shame for ever having proposed marriage to such a monster.

Still, I made it out the other side of that tunnel. I've made it through the collapse of all the other romances and friendships too. Such modern relationship challenges are peanuts compared with the challenges that our ancestors must've worked through, when the DSM-V hadn't been written, a narcissus was still just a flower, and therapy was a word that was centuries away from being invented.

Nobody promised that life would be easy. That's the meaning of it all, I think. The hardships help you to grow, which is what makes it feel like it's all been worthwhile.

PLOTWORKS PUBLISHING

If you enjoyed this book, please leave a review wherever you purchased it.

Then visit Plotworks Publishing to check out J.A. Jernay's companion memoir, *Bold*.

Turn the page for a sneak peek—

J.A. JERNAY

BOLD

a memoir

brief glimpses of a life of risk

THE WASHINGTON POST

My boldest move at The Washington Post occurred on the last Sunday in August.

By this point, I'd been working at the paper for almost a year, and I'd been asked to cover the foreign desk as a weekend aide. This meant that I called foreign correspondents all over the world to bother them about deadlines, to find out when they were going to file their stories. Some editors like to ask those questions themselves, so I just patched them over. Honestly, there really wasn't much to do. Unlike the news desk, the foreign desk gave me time to do my classwork during the shift.

At about nine o'clock that Sunday night, the football-field-sized newsroom was silent. There were literally only three people remaining. Carl, the weekend night editor, was a rambunctious alcoholic from North Carolina who loved the expression *shitfire*. He said it the way other people said *okay*. The second person, Kenny, was the night foreign desk editor; he was mild-mannered and had worked for years at *Stars and Stripes*, the daily American military newspaper read primarily by people overseas.

The third person was me.

I'd just returned from running through the building on my usual route. I'd nodded to all the deaf people working in the third-floor layout area. Post publisher Katharine Graham had hired over a hundred deaf people to put out the paper every night. We communicated mostly through written notes. I'd moved quickly on my usual path through the ground floor printing presses, nodding at the guys in their ink-smudged overalls. We waved at each other a lot, but rarely spoke. The roar of the machines, the lines of newspapers spindling past everywhere, made it impossible to hear, even for the few who weren't deaf.

I'd just sat down in my office chair on the fifth floor again when the foreign desk phone rang.

"I'll get it," said Kenny.

I shrugged. If he wanted to do my job, that was fine. He picked up the phone and listened.

"She *what*?" he suddenly shouted, phone to ear.

I looked over, alarmed. Kenny had literally climbed on top of his chair. He was standing there, his mouth open, phone to ear.

I turned to look at Carl, a short distance away. "What going on?" I said.

"Shitfire, boy, I don't know," he said, straightening up, "but this is gonna be something."

Kenny hung up the phone and turned to both of us. "Princess Diana has been killed," he said.

Neither of them wasted any time. Carl told me to start calling editors at home to come into the newsroom, immediately. I got in touch with three of them; one was already watching the television coverage.

"Listen up," said Kenny to me, his voice tight with urgency. "In a few seconds, you're going to get a call from

Samuel in London. He's going to dictate a piece. You take the dictation and send it straight over to me."

Samuel was the Post foreign correspondent in London. He was one of the few foreign correspondents who I hadn't spoken with.

Quickly I opened a new document on my screen. As I did that, my phone rang.

"Hello," I said.

A man's deep, imperious voice filled my ear. "Begin dictation. On Sunday night, an entire nation was plunged into mourning by the tragic death in an automobile accident of the people's princess, Diana of Wales. At approximately..."

Cradling the phone in my ear, I listened to his voice as my fingers struggled to keep up on the keyboard. I was and still am a fast typist—I can usually hit 70 or 80 words per minute—but this was impossible at that moment. In the late nineties, the Post was still using an awful proprietary software system called RoadRunner. It's long dead now, and at that moment I was wishing for a swift murder. It was lagging badly, and the keys on my computer weren't even pressing down correctly. Plus I was nervous.

After two or three minutes, I had fallen behind Samuel's words. He kept droning on, trying to sound authoritative, but I could also hear him improvising the story too. He used no facts, no numbers, no locations, no cause of death, no quotes, no authorities, no details whatsoever. Diana's death was too new for any of that. He was simply making up vague sentences so we could cram it into the paper for the third edition.

In short, he was bullshitting.

But I was too scared to tell him that I'd lost the thread. So, taking a deep breath, I began to ignore him completely.

Instead, I started typing my own analysis of the death of Princess Diana, which I knew nothing about. I struck a tone of ceremonial sadness and stayed appropriately vague.

In truth, my version wasn't going to be any better or any worse than his. We were equally good with words, and neither one of us knew anything concrete.

At last, Samuel ended the dictation. I hung up the phone. Kenny immediately barked, "Where is it?"

"I have to fix the typos," I said.

"No time!" he said. "Send it right now. It costs five thousand dollars for every ten minutes we hold the presses."

Kenny had literally stopped the presses. And he hadn't done it in the clichéd way you see in television or movies, screaming and foaming at the mouth. He'd just picked up the phone and said it quietly, like a normal person.

The typos had to stay. I immediately sent Kenny the piece. He immediately forwarded it to layout, who immediately poured it onto the front page under a banner headline. Then the powerful presses under the building immediately started printing it, hundreds of thousands of copies.

The next day, *The Washington Post*'s main coverage of the death of Princess Diana was half written by yours truly, under Samuel's name. A college student barely old enough to drink, wearing jeans and sneakers, improvising the way he thought the nation's most important political newspaper ought to memorialize the dead princess of the most important monarchy in the world. Furthermore, with the newspaper's daily circulation of 800,000 at that point, I'd personally committed millions of typos in print.

Nobody ever said anything to me about the piece. Kenny never brought it up. Samuel in London never said anything either. He was too busy doing actual reporting in the following days and weeks. I'm not sure how I benefitted from that moment of high-pressure journalism. The best thing I can say is that I got away with it without getting fired.

Still, I'd been quietly champing at the bit to get my own name in the paper, and it would happen a couple months later.

PLOTWORKS PUBLISHING

Turn the page for a sneak peek of *The Oxford Diaries* by J.A. Jernay!

THE
OXFORD
DIARIES
A STUDENT TRAVELOGUE

J.A. JERNAY

This afternoon, with the energy of a cartoon-hyper, sugared-up toddler, I stepped onto a punt at Magdalen Bridge. Instead of using that wonderous invention called the paddle, Oxonians have instead opted to retain their reputation for efficiency in all pursuits and furnish their boaters with poles. This makes it impossible to push in a straight line. Punts bounce from bank to bank like air hockey disks.

To make a prickly situation even worse, I was pulling the punt from the front—a Cambridge tradition—rather than pushing from the rear in a more Oxford fashion. Such faux pas. Alexandra also did my back a great favor by steering me into a nest of picker bushes.

That night we dined on value meals at KFC with Gerda, then met a Paki friend named Shariq who had a couple bottles of cheap Bulgarian wine, added them to our two bottles of cheap stuff, and traipsed down to the Thames. A full moon, a scenic riverbank, four people, four bottles of alcohol. Nothing but lapping water and happy gulping and tinkling laughter.

Then, in a burst of surrealism, a longboat suddenly cut through the night. It was a party boat sailing down the river, directly before our eyes, from right to left. It carried three hundred brightly-lit partygoers, the drunkest ones hanging off the sides of the boat and whooping like monkeys. "Dancing Queen" by Abba was coming across the water.

Behind the party boat were four teenage boys rowing a skiff in its wake, trying desperately not to lose the party. They saw us, gave up, and paddled over. Docking on the riverbank, they climbed up on the lawn and entertained us for an hour. One taught me the local tradition of punching knuckles together and saying, "Respect!" Another claimed that his older brother's band had just been offered an opening slot for Pearl Jam. Skeptical, I asked for the name, and he said Supergrass. I'd never heard of them. A third told me that my cricket jacket (wool sweater) marks me as a tourist. A fourth one claimed that he wasn't racist because he went to Ireland once.

Finally the boys hopped into the meadow behind us and gamboled about in the bright moonlight like pubescent centaurs.

PLOTWORKS PUBLISHING

Visit Plotworks Publishing today for all these titles—and more!

J.A. Jernay is the author of nearly 80 different works of fiction and nonfiction. He is married to fantasy author A.J. Renwick. He lives in Michigan.

www.ingramcontent.com/pod-product-compliance
Lightning Source LLC
Chambersburg PA
CBHW051831040426
42447CB00006B/469